Language
and
Strategic Inference

Prashant Parikh

LANGUAGE AND STRATEGIC INFERENCE

iUniverse books may be ordered through booksellers or by contacting:

iUniverse
1663 Liberty Drive
Bloomington, IN 47403
www.iuniverse.com
1-800-Authors (1-800-288-4677)

ISBN: 978-1-5320-9006-6 (sc)
ISBN: 978-1-5320-9007-3 (e)

Library of Congress Control Number: 2019920633

Print information available on the last page.

iUniverse rev. date: 12/10/2019

We shall not cease from exploration
And the end of all our exploring
Will be to arrive where we started
And know the place for the first time.

— T. S. Eliot, "Little Gidding"

Praise for *Language and Strategic Inference*

Prashant Parikh's highly original works focus on discourse, adding game theory to the usual mathematical tools linguists and philosophers employ. His approach sheds new light on the interlocking issues of what motivates us to say what we do and how we are understood and misunderstood. New phenomena are discovered, but also new light is shed on old issues such as names and descriptions.

Language and Strategic Inference is Parikh's Stanford dissertation, supervised by Jon Barwise and Ken Arrow. Its publication is welcome, for it provides a good introduction to his three later books and to the rich and growing field of game-theoretic semantics. Philosophers will find the familiar ideas of Russell and Grice and Austin used, analyzed, and deepened in the service of a general and mathematical theory of communication. The book is short and clear and would be an excellent way to bring this new approach into a philosophy of language seminar. It is a source of pride for me that he brings situation semantics into the mix.

— John Perry

Henry Waldgrave Stuart Professor of Philosophy Emeritus, Stanford University

Distinguished Professor of Philosophy Emeritus, University of California, Riverside

Contents

List of Figures

List of Tables

Preface

This book reproduces my doctoral dissertation submitted in 1987 to the Department of Engineering-Economic Systems at Stanford University. It combines two remarkably interesting mathematical frameworks—situation theory and game theory—and applies them to problems in semantics of interest to philosophers, linguists, and computer scientists. (I have cleaned up some punctuation and a bit of the text, corrected a small infelicity and left an oversight intact with a comment in a footnote, and added an index.)

My reading committee consisted of Jon Barwise, a mathematical logician, Kenneth Arrow, a mathematical economist and winner of the 1972 Nobel Memorial Prize in economics, and Ennio Stacchetti, a game theorist. It was the best possible committee for the topic of my dissertation.

The dissertation contains in embryonic form many of the ideas that appear in my later work. These ideas have in part led to a new field of research and to a growing number of researchers interested in applying these frameworks to problems of communication and meaning, and so I thought it would be desirable to make the dissertation publicly available.

— Prashant Parikh
New York City, 2019

1

Introduction

1.1 Meaning and Content

A language is a complex social institution. It is arguable that its primary function is communication. Indeed, it is possible to see language as arising from the communicative needs of a group of interacting agents.[1] This makes it essential to understand what communication is and how it takes place. The framework of situation theory and situation semantics developed by Barwise and Perry (1983) and Grice's (1957, 1969) ideas on nonnatural meaning provide the best starting point for constructing a model of communication.

A trifle paradoxically perhaps, the central fact about most languages is that they are situated. That is, what goes on "outside" the specifically linguistic part of an utterance is at least as important as the linguistic expression itself, if not more. What is communicated in an utterance is a result of the whole utterance, not just the sentence uttered. This makes it possible for different propositions to be communicated in different circumstances even when the same sentence is used. For example, an appropriate utterance of "It's 4 pm" on different days results in quite different propositions being expressed—that it is 4 pm on the day of utterance. This fact, that the same sentence can be used on different occasions to convey different contents, is part of what makes language an efficient system of communication.

The framework developed by Barwise and Perry makes this context-dependence an integral part of utterances. The example we considered above is simple enough. When we generalize this observation to a wider class of utterances, we begin to get an idea of the many diverse ways in which communication can occur. Part of the problem in doing this is that we use language in a relatively natural and un-

---

[1]Lewis (1969), for example, has argued for such a view.

premeditated (or "first-order") way most of the time and it is difficult to detach oneself sufficiently to focus on the factors that make transfers of information possible. A simple device, and a relevant one in the context of current efforts to build intelligent systems, is to ask how such an artificial system might be designed to understand a situated language.[2]

Once we allow contexts a role in the determination of content, it becomes clear that there are certain aspects of utterances that are constant across utterances and others that vary from one situation to another. The most salient linguistic constant is what Barwise and Perry call the meaning of a sentence. When a sentence is used in different circumstances this property of sentences remains constant across utterances. The meaning of a sentence is different from its content in an utterance. We could write a simple schematic equation of the form "(meaning of) sentence + situation of utterance = content." Thus, there is a gap between meaning and content. The meaning of a sentence does not by itself determine the content. Knowing the meaning of a sentence like "It's 4 pm" does not tell us when and where it is 4 pm unless we also know the time and location of utterance.

Part of the task of a theory of communication is to explain how the simple equation stated above comes about, that is, to explain how, given the sentence and utterance situation, a content is determined. If we assume that a language is given, then the problem is to show how we can get from meaning to content. Solving this problem in a completely general way is an extremely difficult task. What we need is a sufficiently general model of the context or the embedding circumstances and of the mechanisms that allow for the flow of information from speaker to addressee.

It is possible to take a step in this direction by bringing in the ideas of game theory and equilibrium developed by von Neumann, Nash, Arrow, Debreu, Aumann and other game theorists and economists. The ideas of rational agency and strategic interaction developed in this tradition provide the remaining part of the framework we need to solve this problem. That is, situation theory plus game theory together provide a sufficient set of tools to tackle this problem, as we will see. Grice's important insights into these issues are what suggest that game-theoretic methods are the right ones to consider in looking at communication. This is further reinforced by Austin's work, in particular, by his emphasis on seeing language as action (see Austin 1975, 1961/1979). These

---

[2]In keeping with this, we will use "agent" and "utterance" and "language" in a relatively abstract way to allow for alternative interpretations of our model in what follows.

ideas, of Austin and Grice, will serve as a backdrop for our efforts to develop a partial model of communication.

One of the key ideas that we get from game theory is the concept of a strategic inference. Grice, and subsequently, Strawson (1964) and Schiffer (1972), have shown how communication involves an extremely complex interplay of inferences about speaker's and addressee's intentions. It turns out that game theory, viewed broadly, provides a mathematical framework for precisely these kinds of inferences.

We turn now to a more precise statement of the problem.

1.2 Communication

We will assume as given a large situation or environment $\mathfrak{E}$. This environment contains, among other things, two rational agents $\mathcal{A}$ and $\mathcal{B}$, who share, among other things, a language $\mathfrak{L}$. $\mathcal{A}$ utters an (indicative) sentence φ (assertively) in an utterance situation u in order to communicate some information p^* to $\mathcal{B}$. Once he has received $\mathcal{A}$'s signal, $\mathcal{B}$'s task is to interpret $\mathcal{A}$'s utterance in interpretive situation i. $\mathcal{A}$ and $\mathcal{B}$ assume common knowledge of their rationality and assume, moreover, that their interaction is a cooperative one.

In general, some aspects of the utterance will be public (see Barwise 1989a). For example, typically, the sentence uttered will be publicly available to both agents after the utterance. Other aspects will, in general, be private, like the goals and intentions of the speaker and addressee. And there may be other aspects of the utterance that are partially shared by $\mathcal{A}$ and $\mathcal{B}$.

The general problem is to find the necessary and sufficient conditions and the precise inferential mechanism by which $\mathcal{A}$ *communicates* some proposition p^* to $\mathcal{B}$. What sentence should $\mathcal{A}$ choose to utter and how should $\mathcal{B}$ interpret this choice of utterance, given their respective goals and information?

The shared language $\mathfrak{L}$ provides shared meanings. Thus, the problem is to show how, under what circumstances, $\mathcal{A}$ and $\mathcal{B}$ can move jointly from meaning to content. As we pointed out above, this is an extremely difficult problem to solve, stated so generally. We outline our approach to it in the next section.

1.3 Strategic Inference

The first task, presumably, is to develop an intuitive picture of communication. We can do this by embedding this problem in the larger picture of flows of information developed by Dretske (1981) and Barwise and Perry (1983). As Barwise and Perry have argued, reality can be viewed as consisting of situations linked to one another by a network of constraints. It is the constraint between two situations that makes one situation carry information about another situation. A smoky situation involves a situation with something on fire. This is the constraint we describe when we say "Smoke means fire." An agent who sees the first situation and who knows the constraint can infer the existence of the second situation. And this agent can pass on this newly acquired information to another agent. Given a group of agents (or distributed system) there will be all kinds of transfers of information. A communication is a special type of flow of information between agents.

The Gricean approach to communication suggests that a transfer of information between two agents will be *communicative* when both the proposition p^* *and the speaker's intention to convey it* become common knowledge as a result of the interaction. This involves both the speaker and addressee jointly inferring various things about each other. We will call this joint two-sided inference a *strategic inference.*

A central thesis of this dissertation is that all transfers of information between agents involve a strategic interaction between them. When the strategic interaction is common knowledge between the agents, that is, when it is a *game* (in the technical sense), the transfer will be communicative.

We will argue for this thesis by developing a detailed account of one strategic inference in isolation. Any complete utterance, that is, any utterance that attempts to express a proposition, will involve many separate acts and strategic inferences. For example, part of a communication will typically involve a referential act, an act of referring to some object, and the communication of this reference to the addressee. Each bit of information communicated will require its own strategic inference(s). Thus, any complete utterance involves an entire system of simultaneous strategic inferences. These inferences have to be simultaneous in general because they codetermine each other in general. For example, an utterance of "Bill has the book" will require inferring the designata of each of the four words in the sentence, (not to mention its internal structure), in order to determine the proposition expressed. No word has any particular priority in this determination. That is, there may be interactions among the various strategic inferences. And the embedding circumstances play a vital role in each inference. Mathematically, this amounts to a system of simultaneous equations.

We begin to see the kinds of complexities involved in even a fairly simple utterance. In general, there will be many Bills around as potential referents, "has" has many different meanings,[3] and there are many different books the speaker might be referring to. Our approach will start by focusing on just one strategic inference in isolation. We will abstract from all the other inferences involved in interpreting an utterance and assume that the addressee has available the partial information obtained from them. Thus, the addressee's problem will be to use this partial information together with the utterance itself to get to the full content communicated.

As an example, we will consider a traditional kind of ambiguity between two possible quantifier orderings and see under what circumstances this might be disambiguated: "Every ten minutes a man gets mugged in New York." This involves a single strategic inference. We will see that a successful strategic inference requires a large number of assumptions about the rationality of the agents involved, their goals and intentions, and their knowledge and beliefs. Not only that, it also involves important assumptions about the language they use, in particular, the kinds of choices the language affords. An important consequence of our analysis is that the content communicated will depend not only on what was uttered but also, crucially, on what the speaker might have uttered but chose not to and on their shared information about these choices.

We will build up the structure of a strategic inference step by step. This will help us to be clear about the assumptions we are making and will also suggest ways in which our construction can be generalized or modified to include the many complexities that we have abstracted from. We will construct this structure, called the Strategic Discourse Model (or simply, *SDM*), from the building blocks of situation theory. The *SDM* will turn out to be a special kind of game that we will call a game of partial information. The content communicated will then be given by the solution to this game, by the Pareto-undominated Nash equilibrium of the game.

Any communication involves at least two things. One is the proposition conveyed and the other is the "force" with which it is conveyed, or as Austin (1961/1979) called it, the *illocutionary* force. In our analysis, we focus first exclusively on the propositional content. Once we have done this, we extend our model to include the illocutionary force of the utterance. This involves a consideration of the appropriate sort of response by the addressee. And with this we get a slightly more complex game that is in important respects similar to the signaling games studied in the field of information economics.

---

[3]The OED lists over 30 entries under "have."

We conclude our analysis by developing a partial mathematical account of the necessary and sufficient conditions for communication. This requires a consideration of more general strategic interactions than have been studied in game theory.

An essential part of our analysis is that this game-theoretic structure is situated somewhere, either in the "minds" of agents or in their ambient circumstances or both. This makes the flow of information a situated communication. An important consequence of this situatedness is that agents are not required to have the potentially infinite set of nested intentions proposed by Grice and others. As Perry (1986a) has argued in the case of belief, the circumstantial nature of action does not require an agent to have every relevant belief explicitly present in their mind. We do not need to consider gravity each time we reach for a glass. In exactly the same way, communicating agents do not need to consider all the relevant intentions explicitly. The ambient game does much of the work. This view of communication, as a situated game, resolves a fair bit of the mystery associated with Gricean analyses of nonnatural meaning regarding how agents with quite finite capacities could ever hope to communicate if it required such inaccessibly complex intentions.

This covers the key points of our approach to the general problem of communication, to the problem of how, given a shared language, communicating agents can get from meaning to content. We turn next to consider some applications of the *SDM*.

1.4 The Strategic Discourse Model

Initially, we developed the *SDM* with a view to modeling the communication of a certain class of implicatures. It turns out, however, that essentially the same sorts of inferences are involved in all communicative flows, for example, those requiring disambiguation or the determination of reference or indirect speech acts.

We can make different assumptions about the utterance situation u and these different assumptions will result in different types, more or less complex, of strategic inferences. The same inferential mechanisms will serve to model flows of different kinds, flows that involve figuring out the reference of a singular term, or disambiguating an ambiguous utterance, or inferring an implicature or speech act, as long as the utterance situations share certain characteristics.

For example, we could assume that $\mathcal{A}$'s goal is common knowledge between $\mathcal{A}$ and $\mathcal{B}$. In such a situation, $\mathcal{B}$ will be able to use his public information of both the language and $\mathcal{A}$'s goal as well as the publicly available aspects of the utterance (like, say, its phonetic properties) to make the intended inferences, whether they involve a disambiguation or an indirect speech act. Such situations, even though relatively simple from a strategic viewpoint, account for the transfer of quite different kinds of information.

Or, we could assume that $\mathcal{A}$'s goal is not known to $\mathcal{B}$, but that the range of possible goals she might have is public. Such situations give rise to more subtle strategic inferences depending on what further assumptions we make. We could, for instance, assume that one of the goals in the above set of goals has a fairly high probability and that this distribution is publicly known, at least approximately.

There are many types of utterance situations and strategic transfers we could consider in this way. In all of these, it will turn out that the assumptions of rationality, cooperation, and public information of the relevant aspects of the discourse situation are necessary and sufficient for the transfer to occur. These are fairly strong assumptions and it may be that in any transfer of information there will always be much additional information that needs to be considered. There is an interesting analogy we can make with what is called the Inventor's Paradox. Often, in proving a proposition, say by mathematical induction, we need to prove something stronger than actually required.[4] Our analysis suggests that communication may be a similar sort of process. Much information that is extraneous to the content per se needs to be considered and becomes available as intermediate information. That is, any communication involves a great deal more than just the communicated content being transferred. This additional information can play an extremely important role in a continuing discourse or sequence of actions because the agents can assume that it is also available without having to communicate it explicitly. This is yet another way in which communication is efficient. This consequence has obvious implications for the design of artificial communicating systems.

The foregoing also suggests that flows of information are probably better classified by classifying the family of sets of assumptions we need to make about discourse situations rather than linguistically or by the particular kind of content being transferred.

With this in mind, we will restrict our analysis to a closer examination of the way in which strategic inferences occur more or less naturally in the use of singular terms, in particular, in establishing the

---

[4]Consider, for example, how one might prove that the sum of the first n odd numbers is a perfect square. The induction step requires us to assume not just that the first n odd numbers sum to a square, but that their sum is in fact n^2. See Barwise (1989b).

reference of a singular term. We will further restrict our analysis to definite descriptions and proper names. Similar mechanisms are involved in disambiguation and in inferring the implicatures and indirect speech acts conveyed by an utterance.

As an application of the *SDM* we will outline a new theory of names and descriptions. It turns out that it is possible to sketch a new account with the aid of the tools of strategic inference and another fundamental relation that we describe below.

1.5   Names, Descriptions, and Reference

Our perspective of strategic inference suggests the possibility of giving a new unified account of names and definite descriptions. This new account involves, in addition to our idea of strategic rationality, an ontological or informational constraint.

Russell (1919) and Strawson (1956) discussed two different ways of using descriptions, the attributive and the referential. Barwise and Perry showed that there are in fact several more ways in which they can be used, and that all the uses they considered could be modeled by treating the interpretation of a definite description as a partial function from situations to individuals. We improve and expand on this model in two ways. Our first claim is that the various uses of descriptions are constrained by what we call an ontological constraint and a communicative constraint. The basic idea underlying the first constraint is that every use of a description is associated with a property. Of course, getting from the linguistic item to the property may itself involve a strategic inference. Properties are the types of entity that can be used to pick out individuals or collections of individuals satisfying the property. This instantiating or extensionalizing is always relative to some external situation, called a resource situation. And properties can be used in other ways too, to determine the property itself or the type of object with that property. The particular logical nature of properties is such that a property can be transformed (relative to some situation) into a related logical entity. And each such way of transforming a property corresponds to a use of the description associated with it. Given an ontology, the range of uses of descriptions is logically constrained by the set of available transforms. We identify six, though a closer scrutiny may reveal more or less. This provides a clearer account of the traditional referential-attributive distinction. Each of these uses is identified with a particular transform and we identify an interesting parallel between ways of specifying sets and ways of specifying individuals.

The second rationality or communicative constraint shows how a particular use can be communicated via a strategic inference. Thus, our account of descriptions is based on these two constraints. These two constraints together determine a relation between the linguistic item, that is the description, and some entity in the world that it picks out. It appears that this fundamental semantical relation is a special case of the more general relation of linguistic representation.

We claim next that names can also be used in different ways, just like descriptions, and that they obey the same constraints. It turns out that with such an account we can solve not just the problem of how communication occurs with names and descriptions but also other semantical problems like the Fregean puzzle of informative identities. This provides something like a communicative approach to such semantical issues. That is, the correct way of viewing such problems is from the point of view of the economics of situated communication.

From this strategic perspective, the problem of names and descriptions requires the addressee to first figure out how the term is being used and then if the use is referential to figure out what the reference is. After we set up this problem, we abstract from the full range of inferences involved and assume that the referential use is given. We then pose the problem of how the reference of a referentially used name or description is mutually established.

Let us look at this problem of establishing reference more closely.

Agents need to be able to refer to various kinds of objects in order to convey information to other agents. Referring to an object is an act in its own right and is typically part of the larger act of uttering an (indicative) sentence (assertively) to communicate some information to an addressee. A referential act is generally only partially observable. A speaker may use, in some situation, the description "the cat" to refer to a particular cat, say, the one on the mat. All that will be directly observable by the addressee, in general at least, is the actual issuing of the locution "the cat." Whether the noun phrase is being used referentially, and who or what the speaker is referring to in so using it, will have to be inferred from other information available to the addressee from the rest of the utterance situation. Referential acts, like many other parts of utterance situations, are, in this sense, at best only partially observable and need to be correctly inferred by addressees in order for certain transfers of information to take place.

Partially observable actions like these can sometimes be more fully understood by an interpreter by taking into account the agent's goals and rationality and the public information that the agent and the interpreter share. If, for example, an agent $\mathcal{A}$ asks another agent $\mathcal{B}$ where the cat is and if B responds with "It's on the mat," the addressee (A in this case) will be able to infer, given the right circumstances, that B is referring to the same object that A was referring to. Intuitively, A is able to do this by assuming that B is rational and is cooperating with A. This assumption allows A to infer B's goal, which is to respond to A's query. Moreover, and crucially, we need to assume that this assumption of rational cooperation and A's inference from it to B's goal is *publicly* available to both A and B. Once the two agents get to public information of B's goal it becomes possible for A, once again on the basis of B's rationality, to infer that B is actually referring to the cat with "it," and this enables A to make sense of B's total utterance, thus resulting in an appropriate transfer of information. Here again, in this step from B's goal to figuring out what B is referring to, it is necessary that the structure of the interaction between A and B be common knowledge. It is necessary that B know the kinds of inferences that A can legitimately make given the situation at hand, and it is necessary that A know that B knows this, and so on to full public information of the relevant part of the strategic interaction between them.

This description indicates how, at least in principle, in many situations where the speaker's goal is publicly available, it may be possible for the addressee to infer what object is being referred to. However, there are several situations in which an agent's goals may not be publicly available, at least fully. In the example above, if we assume there are two or more cats that A may be referring to when she asks B where the cat is, how is the addressee B to know which cat A has in mind? In this case, neither the referential act nor the goal is fully public. The act cannot be fully interpreted without the goal and the goal in turn cannot be determined without interpreting the act, that is, without knowing what A is referring to. This is a situation in which both the speaker's goal and the object she is referring to need to be jointly inferred from the other information available to them in the utterance situation. If we make the same assumptions here of public knowledge of rational cooperation and if we further assume that the range of possible referents of "the cat" (or equivalently, the range of A's possible goals) are publicly known to A and B, then once again we can show that, in several cases, the addressee is able to infer the right reference from this partially observed utterance. Here too, the structure of the strategic interaction between the two agents will need to be public, and, as we might expect, the reasoning involved will be more delicate even though it will not be different from strategic reasoning as such in any fundamental way. As a bonus, however, for the additional effort involved, the addressee will also be able to infer the speaker's goal from the utterance (as inverse strategic information) and this goal will, in fact, become common knowledge between them, and will be available for later use.

Finally, there may be many situations where the reference of a singular term is actually ambiguous or indeterminate and is intended by the speaker to be so. Our assumptions will enable us to give a partial account of such transfers of information as well. Equivalently, we will be able to show when and why, in certain circumstances, a more precise and, in general, more costly locution is called for in order to avoid ineliminable ambiguities in less precise and less costly referential acts.

This sort of account of how references get mutually established can be applied to a wide range of referring terms. Names, pronouns, definite descriptions and even demonstratives can all be handled in a more or less unified way. Finding a set of necessary and sufficient conditions for successful reference is the same problem as finding necessary and sufficient conditions for communicating a reference.

1.6   Plan of the Dissertation

In this dissertation we combine ideas from situation semantics and game theory in what we hope is an enlightening way. We do not attempt to defend or even explain either of these theories in any detail. We start from the realization that each has been a fruitful way of attacking certain problems about information and inference, and hope that by combining them, we will take an important step in developing mathematical tools for the analysis of communication.

In the next chapter we consider one strategic inference in detail and analyze the concept of communication. In Chapter 3 we develop a formal account of the *SDM*. And in Chapter 4 we outline our theory of names and descriptions and consider the problem of reference.

2

Communication and Strategic Inference

2.1 Introduction

In this chapter we will consider one strategic inference in detail. The example we analyze contains a familiar type of ambiguity and we will see how the mechanism of strategic inference enables us to disambiguate the utterance. This will also allow us to introduce informally the terminology that we will be formalizing in the next chapter.

Suppose A, after having picked up the information in a recent report issued by the Muggees Association of New York (i.e. M.A.N.Y.), says to B:

"Every ten minutes a man gets mugged in New York." (φ)

What does A communicate to B by this utterance and how does this communication take place? Without saying something about the circumstances in which the sentence φ is uttered it is impossible to say what gets communicated, if anything, and how it does. We will assume that A wants to give some information about mugging statistics to B and that this goal is common knowledge between them. The problem is that, as stated, the utterance of φ is ambiguous. A could mean either that a particular man gets mugged every ten minutes (call this proposition q) or that some person or other gets mugged every ten minutes (call this p). From a traditional logical perspective, the sentence is ambiguous between two different orderings of the quantifiers. There are, of course, other ways in which φ is ambiguous (e.g. "every ten minutes," "man," "in," "New York"), but our interest is in the ambiguity between p and q. We will assume therefore that it is common knowledge between them that the disjunction $p \vee q$ is "immediately" available to B once φ

is uttered. We will call this disjunctive proposition the *minimal* content of φ in the circumstances described above.

Intuitively, given the circumstances above, we would be inclined to go with the second interpretation. It is difficult to imagine a man as immune to experience as would be required for the truth of q. But this much merely tells us that (in the absence of other relevant shared information to the contrary) the second reading is the one more likely to be true. Under what conditions can B select p over q as the *intended* interpretation with *complete* certainty?

First, note that there *are* circumstances in which q rather than p might be the natural content of an utterance of φ. For example, A and B might be trading stories about the foolishness of men generally, each story being about some particular man. If part of such a conversation, one can imagine that B could, with certainty, interpret A's utterance as conveying q.

In the situation we are looking at, however, it seems plausible to say that we would accept B's inferring p (as the intended content of the utterance) with certainty. In fact, we would be inclined to say rather more than this. We would be willing to say that A succeeds in *communicating p to B*. That is, not only is B able to infer p from the utterance, but the structure of their interaction allows him to infer A's intention to convey p. It also allows A to infer that B can infer p and that B can infer A's intention to convey p. In fact, the structure of their interaction allows both A and B to infer full common knowledge of p and of A's intention to convey p, all with complete certainty. That this suffices for communication is not obvious, and we will show later in this chapter why it does.

How do we account for this disambiguation and the communication of this disambiguated content? As we pointed out in Chapter 1, there are many different factors that play a role in this flow of information. The full structure of the interaction between A and B that accounts for this (familiar type of) communication turns out to be a rather complex affair.

We will make five sets of assumptions about all our discourse situations. The first set will apply to all the situations we consider, more or less, and will be taken for granted unless we explicitly state otherwise. The second set will also apply to all the situations we consider, but they are not quite so general as those in the first set. The third set of assumptions involves more specific assumptions and will vary from circumstance to circumstance. The fourth set contains certain provisional assumptions that would be unnecessary in a more complete model.

The last set we will mention only casually to point out that some such assumptions are needed, without ourselves worrying about the details.

For our first set, we will make six general assumptions called the Communication Assumptions. First, we assume that both $\mathcal{A}$ and $\mathcal{B}$ are rational agents. This means in essence that they choose actions that realize their goals in the best possible way, or in choice-theoretic terminology, they choose actions that maximize their expected payoffs. We also assume that it is common knowledge (or at least a mutual belief) between $\mathcal{A}$ and $\mathcal{B}$ that they are rational.

Second, we will assume that, in the absence of any assumptions to the contrary, agents prefer more relevant information to less, other things being equal. Third, we will assume that agents try to minimize the effort involved in realizing a goal, other things being equal. It may seem that these two assumptions are derivable from the assumption of rationality. In fact, they cannot be; the axioms of rationality admit an extremely broad range of preferences as rational. The first of these two assumptions can however be derived from a more general assumption, (though not one quite so general as rationality), and we will consider this later. The force of these two assumptions is therefore to impose certain restrictions on the kinds of payoffs that agents try to maximize. Both assumptions are also common knowledge between them.

Next, we will assume that the agents cooperate in their communicative efforts. This is a further restriction on the kinds of goals or payoffs that are admissible. Our assumption entails that there is some goal that the speaker and addressee share (at some "level") and that they try to align their preferences or payoffs with this goal, given what they know. We will consider this in detail below. This assumption of cooperation is also public knowledge between them.

Fifth, we assume that $\mathcal{A}$ and $\mathcal{B}$ share a language $\mathcal{L}$. And finally, we will assume that $\mathcal{L}$ is a sufficiently rich or expressive language, one that allows many ordinary propositions to be expressed "minimally." (This is similar to Austin's (1961/1979) notion of the explicit performative and to Searle's (1979) assumption of the existence of a literal paraphrase for a metaphor.)

We will make six assumptions that belong to the "intermediate" set of assumptions. These we will call the Informational Assumptions. The first two assumptions are that the speaker is restricted to uttering sentences whose minimal content is true and relevant, or at least believed to be true and relevant. Both assumptions will be taken to be common knowledge between $\mathcal{A}$ and $\mathcal{B}$. It is certainly possible in general for speakers to say (more precisely, to express "minimally") false or irrelevant things (knowingly). In fact, many interesting implicatures arise in this way. (Irony: "He is a fine friend.") We make these assumptions simply to restrict the domain of inquiry.

Next, we will assume that it is common knowledge that the proposition that $\mathcal{A}$ attempts to communicate is also true and relevant. (That is, we are assuming that both the minimal content and the (intended) content of $\mathcal{A}$'s utterance are true and relevant.) These last two assumptions are reflected in corresponding assumptions we make about the addressee. The addressee will be restricted to making valid and relevant inferences given what he knows or believes, and this too is assumed to be common knowledge.

Our third set of assumptions, the Circumstantial Assumptions, contains, in our particular example, the assumption that $\mathcal{A}$ is attempting to convey some information to $\mathcal{B}$ about mugging statistics in New York and that this is common knowledge between them. We make this assumption to rule out the possibility that $\mathcal{A}$ is communicating some further proposition to $\mathcal{B}$ as an implicature, like apprising him of the diversity of experiences available in NYC. The second assumption is that $\mathcal{A}$'s more specific goal is to communicate p to $\mathcal{B}$ and that this goal is not known to $\mathcal{B}$. And lastly, we will assume that it is common knowledge between them that it is unlikely that there is a particular man who would manage to get mugged every ten minutes.

The fourth set of assumptions, the Minimal Content Assumptions, contains, first, the assumption that the minimal content of an utterance is always directly (that is, without requiring any inferences) available to both $\mathcal{A}$ and $\mathcal{B}$ as common knowledge after $\mathcal{A}$'s utterance. Every communicative act involves a number of (strategic and other types of) inferences. Our purpose is first to isolate a single strategic inference and study it in detail. So we abstract from the other inferential problems and assume that a certain set of possible contents is publicly available to $\mathcal{A}$ and $\mathcal{B}$.

The second provisional assumption is that it is common knowledge between $\mathcal{A}$ and $\mathcal{B}$ that $\mathcal{A}$ wants to convey either the proposition p or the proposition q. Note that this does not follow from our first assumption that the minimal content is publicly available to $\mathcal{A}$ and $\mathcal{B}$. $\mathcal{A}$ could, for example, be wanting to convey the disjunction $p \vee q$ itself (deliberate ambiguity, as often occurs in literature) or perhaps the conjunction $p \wedge q$, as in puns and also sometimes in poetry.

The four sets of assumptions taken together will be called the CICM assumptions. In any real communication there will be many more features of the utterance and its interpretation that will be relevant to the flow. $\mathcal{A}$ and $\mathcal{B}$ will have to be located somewhere, their perceptual situations will need to be specified, and their mode of com-

Communication Assumptions

1. A, B are rational.
2. A, B prefer more information to less, ceteris paribus.
3. A, B prefer lower costs, ceteris paribus.
4. A, B try to cooperate, that is, to align their preferences.
5. A, B share a language $\mathfrak{L}$.
6. $\mathfrak{L}$ is an expressive language.
7. All of the above are common knowledge.

Informational Assumptions

1. The minimal content of A's utterance is true and relevant.
2. The intended content of A's utterance is true and relevant.
3. B is restricted to making valid and relevant inferences.
4. All of the above are common knowledge.

Circumstantial Assumptions

1. A is attempting to convey some information about mugging statistics to B.
2. This is common knowledge between them.
3. A is attempting to convey the proposition p that some person or other gets mugged every 10 minutes.
4. B does not know this.
5. It is common knowledge between A and B that it is very unlikely that there is a particular man who would manage to get mugged every 10 minutes.
6. A utters the sentence φ ["Every ten minutes a man gets mugged in New York."] in discourse situation d.

Minimal Content Assumptions

1. Every utterance can be assumed to have a minimal content relative to the analysis of any particular strategic inference. The minimal content of φ in d is $p \lor q$ (where q is the proposition that a particular man gets mugged every ten minutes).
2. This minimal content is directly, without any inferences, available to A and B as common knowledge.
3. It is common knowledge between A and B that A is attempting to convey either the proposition p or the proposition q.

Unspecified Assumptions

This set of assumptions includes all required assumptions about perception, processing, and the mode of communication.

TABLE 2.1 Summary of Assumptions

munication will have to be considered. Note that $\mathcal{A}$ and $\mathcal{B}$ need not be persons. For our purposes, we will blandly assume that all such required conditions are satisfied, whatever they are. We will call this last unspecified set of assumptions the Unspecified Assumptions.

Our claim then is that if all five sets of assumptions above are satisfied $\mathcal{A}$ will succeed in communicating p to $\mathcal{B}$.

2.2 Games Rational Agents Play

There are at least four difficulties in giving an informal account of a strategic inference. First, strategic inferences just are very complex types of inferences requiring a host of conditions for their validity. Secondly, and perhaps crucially, the process is a nonwellfounded one, in the sense in which logicians (Aczel 1988, Barwise 1989d) use the term. Each agent has to consider what the other agent might do in order to figure out a rational course of action. This requires each agent to consider the fact that the other agent will be taking into account the first agent's possible actions, and so on, ad infinitum. This circularity makes its description difficult, and sometimes also makes it difficult to determine exactly which proposition is the correct one to infer. In our intuitive account we will stick to the main story and return later to justify certain tentative statements made along the way. Thirdly, the structure we will develop turns out to be different from the traditional structures studied under the rubric of games of incomplete information. So, although we will be using the tools of game theory our model will not be a straightforward application of these tools and will require us to build a new type of game, a game of *partial* information, from scratch.

And lastly, there is the problem of how we are to interpret the game-theoretic structure we will construct. It would be plainly absurd to claim that people explicitly carry out all the "steps" involved in a strategic inference. We will instead see the game of partial information as a model of an important subclass of a large class of constraints that might be said to capture the underlying structure or logic of language and communication. Just as *modus ponens* describes the conditions for a legitimate deductive inference in traditional (that is, "unsituated") logic without implying that an agent necessarily uses it explicitly to arrive at a warranted conclusion, so our model describes the structure of a valid strategic inference in a "situated" logic (Barwise 1989b) without implying anything about the actual procedures used by agents to arrive at the correct interpretation of an utterance. However, we will often talk as if agents are actually performing the various tasks involved because this makes the model more accessible from an intuitive point of view.

(How persons actually communicate is an interesting problem and the idea of pattern matching may have something to contribute here, the patterns being different classes of games perhaps.)

To start with, we have a situation d that we will call the discourse situation in which the transfer of information takes place. We can extract two component situations u and i from this discourse situation called, respectively, the utterance situation and the interpretive situation. The utterance situation is, as one might expect, the situation in which $\mathcal{A}$ utters φ, and the interpretive situation is the situation in which $\mathcal{B}$ attempts to interpret $\mathcal{A}$'s utterance. In a more complete model we would need a third situation r, called the reception situation, in which the addressee picks up or receives or perceives the utterance. In keeping with our last (Unspecified) set of assumptions above we will abstract from problems of perception and reception and so will not consider the reception situation r explicitly.

If the attempted communication is successful, $\mathcal{B}$ will presumably interpret φ (in d) as p. We will also assume that d (and therefore u and i) is embedded in a larger situation B—called the background—which is itself part of a situation $\mathfrak{E}$, called the environment, in which all events of interest occur. The Communication and Information Assumptions will be assumed to hold in B and the Circumstantial Assumptions to hold in d.

The utterance situation u has in it, among other things, $\mathcal{A}$ and $\mathcal{B}$, with $\mathcal{A}$ saying φ to $\mathcal{B}$. We need to start by considering why $\mathcal{A}$ chooses to say φ. This is a complex matter and, as we will see, one side of the coin whose other side will turn out to be an account of why $\mathcal{B}$ chooses (in i) to interpret φ in u as p. It is this dual choice that will be seen to constitute the joint act of communication.

The natural place to start if we wish to consider $\mathcal{A}$'s choice of φ is with $\mathcal{A}$'s goal. She wants to communicate p to $\mathcal{B}$. Presumably, the language $\mathfrak{L}$ provides a number of sentences that will do the job in the assumed circumstances. One of them may be φ. The minimal content $(p \lor q)$ of φ is certainly both true (or at least believed to be true) and relevant to $\mathcal{A}$'s goal. (The Muggees Association of New York (i.e. M.A.N.Y.) has never been known to exaggerate.) Since $\mathfrak{L}$ is a "rich" language $\mathcal{A}$ could also choose to utter a sentence ψ_1 whose minimal content (in d) is p. This might be, for example, a sentence like "Every ten minutes some man or other gets mugged in New York." $\mathcal{A}$ has thus at least two ways to attempt to convey p. We could imagine others and collect them all together in a set called the choice set of $\mathcal{A}$. This set of sentences (and more generally of actions) is known, strictly speaking, only to $\mathcal{A}$. Of course, $\mathcal{B}$ would know that it must be some subset of $\mathfrak{L}$, but this is obviously not very helpful (especially since $\mathfrak{L}$ is a rich language). In general, $\mathcal{B}$ cannot be assumed to know what $\mathcal{A}$ believes to be true and relevant. Besides, we do not need to make the implausible assumption that $\mathcal{A}$ considers all the sentences of $\mathfrak{L}$ that will express true propositions that are relevant to her goal. $\mathcal{A}$ is a finite agent and consequently can be said to consider only small subsets of its possible choice set. So, let's say that $\mathcal{A}$ has a choice set that contains φ, ψ_1, and perhaps other sentences that could be used to express true and relevant propositions (minimally and otherwise).

As a rational agent $\mathcal{A}$ needs to consider her choices, evaluate the possible consequences of uttering each of them, and then choose the best course of action. Let's start by considering the possible consequences of uttering φ. $\mathcal{B}$ is faced with the task of choosing a proposition as the intended interpretation of φ in u. As far as $\mathcal{B}$ is concerned $\mathcal{A}$ could be communicating either p or q. We could say that $\mathcal{A}$'s utterance of φ raises the issue for $\mathcal{B}$ whether p or q is being communicated. $\mathcal{B}$ has no prior way of settling this issue, given what he knows. This situation can be modeled by the graph in Figure 2.1.

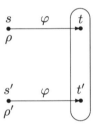

FIGURE 2.1 Stage One of Local Game $LG(\varphi)$

The two initial nodes s and s' represent the two possible ways of settling the issue of whether $\mathcal{A}$'s intention is to communicate p or q. Each initial node can be thought of as a situation that contains the relevant state of affairs together with other facts. Thus, in s we have $\mathcal{A}$ intending to convey p among other things, and in s' we have her intending to convey q. Note that $\mathcal{A}$ knows she is in s and not in s'. But all $\mathcal{B}$ knows, and knows only *after* $\mathcal{A}$ has uttered φ, is that $\mathcal{A}$ could be either in s or in s'. In any case, $\mathcal{A}$'s uttering φ is compatible with both s and s', given our Information Assumptions above. The branches at the first level of the tree represent this action by $\mathcal{A}$. Performing this action in u gets $\mathcal{A}$ from the situation s to the new situation t and performing it on s' gets $\mathcal{A}$ to the situation t'. Once again, $\mathcal{A}$ knows that uttering φ

would result in t, but $\mathcal{B}$ is unable to distinguish between t and t'. We represent this inability on $\mathcal{B}$'s part by an oval containing t and t' and we will say that t and t' belong to the same "information set" for $\mathcal{B}$. This is $\mathcal{B}$'s situation after he perceives φ.

We made the Circumstantial Assumption above that it is common knowledge between $\mathcal{A}$ and $\mathcal{B}$ that p is much more likely to be true than q. In the absence of any further information to the contrary, we can suppose that (as a consequence of this assumption) $\mathcal{A}$ and $\mathcal{B}$ will take it to be common knowledge between them that $\mathcal{A}$ is much more likely to be attempting to convey p rather than q. We have represented this shared knowledge that s is more likely to be the case than s' by the probabilities $\rho = 0.9$ and $\rho' = 0.1$ respectively. The particular numerical values are unimportant as long as the one is greater than the other. Note that, in general, there is a big difference between the likelihood of a proposition's being true and the likelihood of an agent intending to convey that proposition. It is the absence of further relevant information that justifies our identifying the two probabilities.[1]

As we said above, $\mathcal{B}$ has to choose an appropriate interpretation at this point. He has the same two choices of proposition at t and t' as shown in Figure 2.2. He could choose either p or q.

If $\mathcal{B}$ is in t then the intended interpretation is p and it is clear that this is what he should choose. And if he is in t' it is intuitively clear that he should choose q. Unfortunately, $\mathcal{B}$ has as yet no clue about which situation he is in, he knows only that he is either in t or in t'.

Because $\mathcal{B}$ cannot tell where he is in the tree it is not clear what his best choice should be as the optimal action is different for t and t'. Note that our last Circumstantial Assumption allows $\mathcal{B}$ to think that it may be more likely that $\mathcal{A}$ is communicating p and that this is common

---

[1]The full story is a little more intricate than we have indicated. We have not spelled out (in the last Circumstantial Assumption) the universe of propositions in which q is assumed to be unlikely. It would be wrong to assume that this universe is $\{p, q\}$ because this set comes to be common knowledge only after $\mathcal{A}$ has uttered φ. Informally, we might say that $\mathcal{A}$'s utterance of φ gives $\mathcal{B}$ the information that either p or q is being conveyed (by the second Minimal Content Assumption above). Then $\mathcal{B}$ can infer that, of the two, q is much less likely to be true than p. In other words, $\mathcal{B}$ can derive conditional probabilities for p and q, given the proposition $p \vee q$. The underlying universe over which this conditioning is done will be some larger (unspecified/indeterminate) set of propositions. Once $\mathcal{B}$ gets conditional probabilities for p and q, he can, in the absence of further relevant information, more or less identify these probabilities with the corresponding conditional probabilities that $\mathcal{A}$ is attempting to convey p or to convey q, given that $\mathcal{A}$ is attempting to convey either p or q. Finally, all this is common knowledge, getting us to the represented probabilities above.

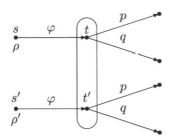

FIGURE 2.2 Stage Two of Local Game $LG(\varphi)$

knowledge between them. But this additional information still does not help him to eliminate the uncertainty involved.

$\mathcal{A}$ of course knows that it is the situation t that results from her utterance of φ. But $\mathcal{A}$ also knows that for $\mathcal{B}$ t and t' are in the same information set. In fact, it is easy to see that the CICM assumptions imply that the information represented by the tree above becomes common knowledge between them once $\mathcal{A}$ utters φ.

We indicated above that it was intuitively clear what choices $\mathcal{B}$ should make in the two situations t and t', but that he is unable to figure out the optimal course of action because t and t' are indistinguishable to him. We can make this intuition precise by developing an informal account of $\mathcal{A}$'s and $\mathcal{B}$'s payoffs or preferences. The basic idea is that after both $\mathcal{A}$ and $\mathcal{B}$ make their choices and perform their optimal actions they get some satisfaction or payoff from their actions in the resulting situation. If the actions come close to fulfilling their goals their payoffs will be relatively high.

We note first that it is common knowledge that $\mathcal{B}$ has partial knowledge of $\mathcal{A}$'s goal, that she is conveying either the proposition p or the proposition q. Next, we note that p and q are both individually more informative than just $p \vee q$, and moreover are also relevant to $\mathcal{A}$'s goal above. If $\mathcal{A}$ is communicating p then, given our Communication Assumptions, we can certainly deduce that the payoff (to $\mathcal{B}$) for $\mathcal{B}$'s choosing p is higher than the payoff for choosing $p \vee q$. We could assume that the costs involved in transmitting and inferring these two propositions are roughly the same. But in this very situation t, q would not yield a higher payoff because the flow would not be informational. Thus, given t (or s), we would have the payoff ordering $v(s, \varphi, q) < v(s, \varphi, p \vee q) < v(s, \varphi, p)$. It is easy to see that the ordering would be reversed for the situation t' because now p would make the flow misinformational rather than q.

There is an important question we need to address at this point about these two orderings. Is there more information available that allows us to strengthen the ordering in any way? This question is just an instance of the important debate (in economics, primarily) about cardinal, ordinal, and von Neumann-Morgenstern (N-M) utility functions. We will assume that it is possible to strengthen the orderings above into an N-M utility function. This implies that each payoff can be assigned numerical values, and that all (positive) linear transformations of the payoff function are equivalent. (That is, if v is a payoff function, then we can equivalently use any function $v' = av + b$, $a > 0$, without changing the game.)

What justifies this further assumption? To begin with, there is implicit in the situation we are looking at the information that, at least roughly, $v(s, \varphi, p) = v(s', \varphi, q)$. As far as $\mathcal{B}$ knows, $\mathcal{A}$ has no reason to derive greater satisfaction from conveying p rather than q or vice-versa. Misinformation should also carry the same degree of dissatisfaction, independently of the particular misinformation conveyed, at least in the situation we are looking at. This implies that $v(s, \varphi, q) = v(s', \varphi, p)$. Though these assumptions are appropriate for our particular game (that is, relative to the Circumstantial Assumptions), it should be evident that there will be many discourse situations in which these assumptions will not hold. But there will be different assumptions that will hold in such circumstances and these will suggest appropriate quantitative assessments. However, these equalities (or inequalities, as the case may be) do not contain information that allows us to strengthen the ordinal utility functions to an N-M utility function. We can also make the additional plausible assumption that information should be valued quite highly over misinformation. How much more becomes relevant when we consider values for costs of transmitting particular messages. In general, the cost of an utterance and its corresponding interpretation should be much smaller than the satisfaction or dissatisfaction derived from the content of an utterance. This is a reasonable assumption in many ordinary discourse situations but, again, certainly not in all situations. It is this assumption of relative magnitudes of costs and satisfactions and dissatisfactions that gives us the additional information that justifies our use of N-M utility functions.

Let us, for the sake of concreteness, assign numbers to these payoffs in accord with our observations above, say plus 10 for the additional information and minus 10 for the misinformation. (Note that any positive linear transformation of this function will do equally well.)

These payoffs can then be represented on our tree in the obvious way in Figure 2.3.

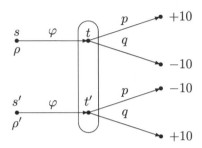

FIGURE 2.3 Stage Three of Local Game $LG(\varphi)$

This representation now makes $\mathcal{B}$'s dilemma quite clear. He cannot tell which of t and t' is factual and the payoffs are symmetric and conflicting. If he were to choose p, then he would get a payoff of 10 if the situation he was in turned out to be t. But if t' were factual he would end up with a minus 10. And the same problem crops up with a choice of q. If he were to choose one or the other randomly, say by tossing a (fair) coin, he would get an expected payoff of 0, certainly much lower than his maximum possible payoff!

So far, we have referred to the function v as $\mathcal{B}$'s payoff function. The ordering was derived, however, from knowledge that is shared by $\mathcal{A}$ and $\mathcal{B}$, from CICM and from shared partial information about $\mathcal{A}$'s goal. This makes the ordering itself common knowledge and, given our fourth Communication Assumption of cooperation, we can assume that both $\mathcal{A}$ and $\mathcal{B}$ have the same ordering. In fact, the ordering reflects both $\mathcal{A}$'s goal of communicating p and $\mathcal{B}$'s goal to cooperate in interpreting $\mathcal{A}$'s utterance. Note that it is because this cooperation is common knowledge and because the other assumptions as well as the inference to partial information about $\mathcal{A}$'s goal are also common knowledge that the ordering also becomes available as common knowledge. We will assume further, to keep things simple, that $\mathcal{A}$ and $\mathcal{B}$ also agree on the particular numbers that we have assigned to the various values.

It seems plausible to say (on the basis of this account at least) that if there was nothing else to the discourse situation it would not be possible for $\mathcal{B}$ to disambiguate φ in d.[2] For this to be possible it is necessary for $\mathcal{B}$ to take into account the fact that $\mathcal{A}$ is a rational

---

[2] *My current comment*: This observation is incorrect because a simple Nash equilibrium would have solved this problem. But this oversight was productive in that

agent and therefore that $\mathcal{A}$ has acted optimally in choosing to utter φ. In order to figure out what makes φ $\mathcal{A}$'s optimal choice $\mathcal{B}$ needs to consider what $\mathcal{A}$ might have said but chose not to.

Even though $\mathcal{B}$ cannot know all the choices available to $\mathcal{A}$ he shares with $\mathcal{A}$ the fact that $\mathfrak{L}$ is a rich language and therefore that there is at least one sentence in $\mathfrak{L}$ whose minimal content in d is p, and also that there is a sentence that will express q minimally. To keep things simple we will assume that, in the case of p, this sentence is the same as ψ_1 above. For q we can assume that there is a sentence ψ_2, say, "Every ten minutes a particular man gets mugged in New York," whose minimal content in d is q. Here too, we will assume that both $\mathcal{A}$ and $\mathcal{B}$ consider the same sentence ψ_2 even though the assumption is not strictly necessary.

This enables $\mathcal{B}$ to construct the model depicted in Figure 2.4 of the structure of their interaction once $\mathcal{A}$ has said φ.

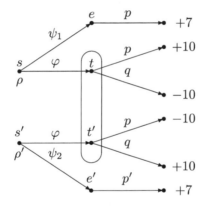

FIGURE 2.4 Local Game $LG(\varphi)$

We note in passing that the two actions involving ψ_1 and ψ_2 satisfy our Information Assumptions.

We need to account for the payoffs assigned to the two new paths in the tree above. Given s, the only difference between $v(s, \varphi, p)$ and $v(s, \psi_1, p)$ lies in the costs involved and, given our Communication Assumption of least effort, it is reasonable to say that $v(s, \psi_1, p) < v(s, \varphi, p)$. Also, the additional cost involved in this longer and more specific sentence is small relative to the difference between information

---

it led to interesting considerations of Pareto-Nash equilibria, which proved to be very useful later, especially in Parikh (2019).

and misinformation, as we pointed above. We will, once again for the sake of concreteness, assume that this payoff is assigned the number 7. The same reasoning goes through for the path with ψ_2 and we set $v(s', \psi_2, q) = 7$.

This is B's model of the structure of A's and B's interaction. But we can now note that it was constructed from their shared knowledge so that the entire structure is in fact available to both A and B (to B only after φ has been uttered). This makes the structure itself common knowledge between them (also only after φ has been uttered). We will call this structure $LG(\varphi)$. $LG(\varphi)$ is a new type of game that we will call a game of partial information. We will also call it a local game because it will turn out to be part of a larger structure called a global game. Thus, $LG(\varphi)$ is a local game of partial information.

We started this discussion with a view to looking at the possible consequences of A's uttering φ in d. We now have part of the answer to this question. Upon uttering φ, B will construct $LG(\varphi)$ to represent the structure of their interaction. A is also able to construct $LG(\varphi)$ (she can in fact construct it before she actually utters φ). And finally, $LG(\varphi)$ becomes common knowledge between them (after the utterance).

$LG(\varphi)$ is the choice structure that now confronts B and is therefore the structure that A needs to consider before she actually chooses φ. Is there enough information in $LG(\varphi)$ for B to eliminate t' as a possible situation he is in and so be able to choose p? This is B's problem. But it is also therefore A's problem because A's optimal choice will depend in part on whether B has enough information to solve this problem.

We will show later that it is possible for B to eliminate t' from his information set. The argument for this is intricate and it seems best to discuss it after we give a complete account of the choice structure that A and B face. For now, let's assume that B is able to figure out that he is not in t' and therefore that he is able to choose p as his preferred interpretation. Since $LG(\varphi)$ is common knowledge between them A has access to this reasoning. In fact, the solution process is also common knowledge between them, and A is justified in anticipating B's choice of p and so they can both receive a payoff of 10. We will say that the value of the game $LG(\varphi)$, $v[LG(\varphi)]$, is 10. In other words, if A chooses to say φ then A and B will both receive a payoff of 10.

The choice structure that A faces is now easy to see. For every ψ A has in her choice set there is a corresponding local game $LG(\psi)$. For example, $LG(\psi_1)$ is the trivial game in Figure 2.5.

$LG(\psi_1)$ clearly has a value of 7.

$$s \quad \psi_1 \quad t \quad p$$

$$+7$$

FIGURE 2.5 Local Game $LG(\psi_1)$

$\mathcal{A}$'s choice problem is now easy to state. She has to choose the sentence ψ that yields the highest value $v[LG(\psi)]$. We can represent this problem as in Figure 2.6.

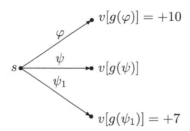

$$v[g(\varphi)] = +10$$

$$s \xrightarrow{\psi} v[g(\psi)]$$

$$v[g(\psi_1)] = +7$$

FIGURE 2.6 Global Game GG

If we assume that $\mathcal{A}$ considers only φ and ψ_1 then it is clear that her optimal action is to utter φ. We will call this larger structure (in which the various local games can be said to be embedded) the global game (of partial information) and denote this by GG. We have implicitly assumed of course that every local game $LG(\psi)$ has a value and this is something we will have to justify later.

But we now have a reasonably complete picture of the structure of the interaction between $\mathcal{A}$ and $\mathcal{B}$ that makes it possible for $\mathcal{A}$ to communicate p to $\mathcal{B}$. We will call this structure which includes both the global and the local games the strategic discourse model or, simply, the *SDM*.

We started by considering why $\mathcal{A}$ chooses to say φ. And we have given an account of $\mathcal{A}$'s choice problem that shows why φ is $\mathcal{A}$'s optimal choice. In so doing we have simultaneously accounted for why p turns out to be the optimal interpretation for $\mathcal{B}$ to pick once he has heard φ. In fact, as we said above, it is the joint optimality of their choices that makes them individually optimal. It is this dual, "two-sided" optimizing, or what is called strategic rationality, that makes communication possible.

It is important to point out an important asymmetry in this strategic discourse model, however. $\mathcal{B}$ gets to consider only one local game, the one constructed from $\mathcal{A}$'s (optimal) choice. $\mathcal{A}$, on the other hand, has to consider all the local games issuing from the sentences in her choice set and then choose to play the one with the maximal value. It is not necessary for B to make conjectures about all the possible things A might have said but did not.

It is now time to justify the two provisional statements we made along the way. The first and major one concerns the kind of reasoning that B (and A) can employ to eliminate the possibility that B is in t' (if he receives φ). Expressed game-theoretically, we have to show how A and B can "solve" the game $LG(\varphi)$. The second has to do with the existence of a value for every game $LG(\psi)$ that A might consider.

2.3 Solving Games Rational Agents Play

Before we turn to solving $LG(\varphi)$ it is worth making a general distinction in the context of our game-theoretic analysis. It is important to distinguish between the model $LG(\varphi)$, the different sorts of interactions $LG(\varphi)$ could be a model of, and consequently the different ways in which the model could be analyzed. A similar distinction is explicitly made by Aumann (1985) and also by Kreps (1987). We have already made it implicitly by separating our account of the model from our account of how this model is to be analyzed.

Solving a game involves finding a pair of "strategies" (one for each player in a two-player game) that is in some sense optimal. It appears that there are many ways to solve the same abstract game, each way being more or less appropriate depending on the particular interpretation we give to the game. A solution concept that may seem appealing in an economic or political context may not be as appealing in a discourse situation; even two different economic contexts or two different discourse situations may provide different grounds for accepting or rejecting a proposed solution.

One persistent problem with many solution concepts is the existence of multiple solutions.[3] This multiplicity is troublesome in most situations because if two or more strategy pairs are optimal then players may not know which strategy to play and choosing different or nonmatching optima may result in a suboptimal outcome.

To take Schelling's example (1960), if two people have to meet in New York and are not in a position to communicate with each other, any place in the city would do as long as they both choose the same spot. This is a (coordination) game with multiple "solutions." But such solutions are obviously not particularly helpful in prescribing a course of action. Of course, in situations like these, in the absence of other rele-

---

[3]This is an important part of the reason why so many solution concepts have been investigated.

vant information (perhaps both players are natives and this is common knowledge between them making Grand Central Station a "salient" spot; or it is common knowledge that they are both tourists which might make the Empire State Building "focal") one should not expect unique solutions. In fact, Lewis (1969) uses this nonuniqueness as a necessary condition in the definition of conventions. It is the existence of multiple rational ways of doing something that makes it worthwhile for the players involved to agree on a convention. But it turns out that most solution concepts also allow many unintuitive and implausible solutions to slip past their restrictions, at least under some interpretations of the abstract game under consideration. Exactly which (and how many) solutions are intuitively warranted in a game seems to depend on other features of the particular context being modeled.[4]

We made the distinction above to keep open the possibility of using different solution concepts for the same local game $LG(\varphi)$. The solution concept we will use combines one of the more popular solution concepts called a Nash equilibrium with the idea of Pareto-dominance.

To spell out the concept of a Nash equilibrium we first need to say what a strategy is. A strategy is essentially a function from the set of all the decision nodes of a player to a set of actions. It is a prescription of what a player will do at any node in the game tree where it is her turn to act. For example, the function $\{(s, \varphi), (s', \varphi)\}$ is one of A's strategies in the game $LG(\varphi)$. A has only two possible choice situations and a strategy specifies her choices in both of them. It is easy to see that A has exactly four strategies in this game. It is important to note that a strategy for A involves a specification of what she would do in s' even though she knows that s' isn't factual. This is necessary because B needs to consider what A might do in s' and so A needs to consider what B might do if he takes into account the possibility that A might be choosing an action in s'.

B's strategies involve a slight complication and with it a small refinement of the rough definition of strategy we gave above. B has four choice situations to consider t, t' and e, e'. Since t and t' belong to the same information set, B cannot distinguish between the two and so B's choices at t and t' will have to be constrained to be the same. That is, the correct domain for the strategy of a player is not the set

---

[4]In many discourse situations nonuniqueness has in fact a different sort of interpretation, making possible the extraction of information not otherwise available. If a local game has multiple solutions and if A chooses to play it then some sort of ambiguity is left unresolved in the communication and this may convey to the addressee that the ambiguity was intentional for some reason or other (depending on context). We will consider this and other such information later.

of all decision nodes but the set of all the information sets. In $\mathcal{A}$'s case, the domain of a strategy will contain the singleton information sets $\{s\}$ and $\{s'\}$.

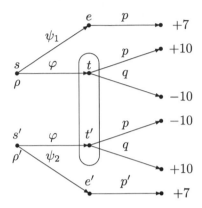

FIGURE 2.7 Local Game $LG(\varphi)$

Let us list the strategies of both players. $\mathcal{A}$ has the following four strategies:

$$
\begin{array}{llll}
1. & s \mapsto \phi, & s' \mapsto \psi_2 & = (\phi, \psi_2) \\
2. & s \mapsto \phi, & s' \mapsto \phi & = (\phi, \phi) \\
3. & s \mapsto \psi_1, & s' \mapsto \phi & = (\psi_1, \phi) \\
4. & s \mapsto \psi_1, & s' \mapsto \psi_2 & = (\psi_1, \psi_2)
\end{array}
$$

And $\mathcal{B}$ has the following two strategies:

$$
\begin{array}{llll}
1. & e \mapsto p, & t, t' \mapsto p, & e' \mapsto q & = (p, p, q) = p \\
2. & e \mapsto p, & t, t' \mapsto q, & e' \mapsto q & = (p, q, q) = q
\end{array}
$$

We can simplify the notation if we agree on a convention that specifies the information sets of a player in some predefined order, say, from top to bottom with respect to the tree. This would get us to the simpler forms given above. To interpret an ordered pair like $\langle \varphi, \psi_2 \rangle$ one has to go back to the tree and figure out which action is prescribed where. We can further simplify the representation of $\mathcal{B}$'s strategies by explicitly mentioning only those decisions that represent a "real" choice. Thus, $\mathcal{B}$'s choices are constrained to be p and q at e and e' respectively, so we need not mention these explicitly. Note that we have already made an implicit simplification in our specification of the strategy functions above. The values of the two functions have been represented as either sentences or propositions. They are actually the corresponding actions, either of uttering the sentence in question or of interpreting the uttered sentence as expressing the relevant proposition.

If a is a strategy of $\mathcal{A}$'s and b of $\mathcal{B}$'s then the pair $\langle a, b \rangle$ is a strategy in the game. (Strategies in games are sometimes also called strategy profiles.) This gives us exactly eight strategies in the game $LG(\varphi)$ above. These eight strategies constitute our strategy space. Intuitively, the unique solution that we expect in this game is the pair $\langle \varphi, \psi_2, p \rangle$.

What we have defined above is the concept of a *pure* strategy (for players and in the game). In general, players will be able to "mix" strategies by randomizing on their pure strategy sets. In other words, a mixed strategy of a player is a probability distribution on its set of pure strategies. And the full space of strategies is the set of ordered pairs of probability distributions, one for each of the two players. The argument we give below can be easily extended to this larger space and so we will stick to the smaller set of eight pure strategies to focus on its essential points. Unless we say otherwise, strategy will henceforth mean pure strategy.

A strategy is a Nash equilibrium if no player has an incentive to deviate unilaterally from this strategy. Unilateral deviation by a player is deviation keeping the strategies of other players fixed. In our case of two players the criterion is relatively simple to apply. Consider the strategy $\langle \psi_1, \psi_2, p \rangle$. $\mathcal{B}$ certainly has no incentive to deviate from p to q—it makes no difference which of the two he chooses because $\mathcal{A}$'s strategy doesn't allow the information set $\{t, t'\}$ to become factual. But if $\mathcal{A}$ deviates unilaterally, (that is, keeping $\mathcal{B}$'s choice of p fixed), to the strategy $\langle \varphi, \psi_2 \rangle$ then she certainly does better. That is, $v(\varphi, \psi_2, p)$ is greater than $v(\psi_1, \psi_2, p)$. This eliminates the original strategy $\langle \psi_1, \psi_2, p \rangle$ from the set of Nash equilibria. A quick run through the strategy space will show that of the eight strategies only two qualify as Nash equilibria. These are $\langle \varphi, \psi_2, p \rangle$ and $\langle \psi_1, \varphi, q \rangle$. Let us call these N_1 and N_2.

This is probably the most widely used solution concept in the theory of (noncooperative) games. It is worth pointing out though that this criterion cannot be directly deduced from the axioms of utility theory that characterize the behavior of individual rational agents (see Bernheim 1984, Brandenburger and Dekel 1985). Its plausibility lies in its being a necessary condition for rationality if it is already assumed a priori by the players that some rational prescription for action exists in the game. Such an assumption is not always warranted and this has been part of the motivation behind recent efforts to provide more basic foundations for solution concepts (Aumann 1987, Kreps 1987).[5]

We will use the Nash criterion without further justification here. We still have to face the fact that there are two Nash equilibria N_1 and N_2 only one of which is intuitively plausible. We need to impose further conditions that a solution must satisfy that make it possible to discriminate between N_1 and N_2.[6]

To solve this multiple equilibrium problem, we need to bring in the idea of Pareto-dominance. It says simply that of two strategies in a game, if one results in higher payoffs for all players concerned, the other can be eliminated. Though this appears to make perfect intuitive sense there is a problem with it because it implicitly assumes some degree of correlated action (deviation) between players, something that requires additional assumptions to be warranted in a noncooperative game. In fact, there is often a conflict between the Nash criterion and the Pareto-dominance criterion (as evinced, for example, by the Prisoner's Dilemma).

We will use Pareto-dominance as a second-order criterion. First, we determine the set of Nash equilibria. Then we apply the Pareto criterion to this set. This ensures that all our solutions will satisfy the important Nash property that there is no incentive to deviate from a possible equilibrium strategy. That, after all, is what justifies our calling it an "equilibrium" strategy. And this second-order way of using it to eliminate counterintuitive Nash equilibria (and their refinements) is easier to justify. There is also an important general point to be made in justifying this hybrid solution concept and we will develop it at some length in a footnote.[7]

---

[5]Aumann, in particular, has shown that it is possible to deduce the weaker concept of correlated equilibrium from common knowledge of rationality and from the assumption that has come to be called the Harsanyi Doctrine.

[6]Though we will not go into the details here it seems important to point out that none of the standard refinements of Nash equilibrium (sequential, perfect, and proper equilibria, (iterated) dominance, the intuitive criterion, divinity and universal divinity) help here because they all have force by imposing restrictions on "out-of-equilibrium" beliefs. See Kreps (1986). N_2 is also a stable equilibrium so the stability requirements of Kohlberg and Mertens (1986) do not help here either. An interesting alternative is to see the game as a team-theoretic problem. But solving team problems requires communication among the players. In our case, allowing for preplay communication runs into either or both of two problems. First, there is the danger of an infinite regress because our problem is itself a communication problem. And second, even if such an infinite regress were avoidable, the solution would certainly require a great deal of effort suggesting that languages aren't quite so efficient as they in fact are.

[7]As Schelling (1960), most notably, has pointed out, noncooperative games have payoffs that can be thought of (at least loosely) as lying along a continuum ranging

from games of pure coordination to games of pure conflict. Intuitively, a game of pure coordination is one in which all players have "perfectly aligned interests," and a game of pure conflict is one in which they have "strictly opposed interests." A sufficient condition for a game to be a pure coordination game is that the payoffs of all players be identical. (It is easy to define a necessary and sufficient condition, but it is unnecessary here.) For a game of pure conflict, it turns out that only two-person zero-sum games can have payoffs with strictly opposed interests. Most games lie in between these two extremes: their payoffs reflect a mix of conflict and coordination, and they are, predictably, called mixed-motive games. The term *noncooperative* that is used to describe this entire class of games refers not to the "interests" of the players but to the conditions and constraints under which they have to choose a rational course of action. Noncooperative games are models of situations in which no *"binding* agreements" are possible. Cooperative games admit binding agreements between players and it is this element that makes them "cooperative" games, resulting in the possibility of coalition-based behavior (Aumann 1976).

The evolution of game theory seems to suggest an implicit bias against an appreciation of the element of coordination that is present in most noncooperative games. All the solution concepts that have been explored appear to focus exclusively on the possibilities for conflictual (or, in ordinary language, noncooperative) behavior. Fully rational behavior should, at least intuitively, reflect both caution against possible conflictual behavior by other players as well as the extraction of possibilities for coordination (informally, cooperation). And the solution concepts we define should capture both sets of possibilities. To be sure, the recent literature shows how subtle considerations of strategic interactions can be. But I'm tempted to think that most game theorists would agree that it is a problem that we do not have a solution concept that gives us the obvious unique solution to the following pure coordination game:

x, x	$0, 0$
$0, 0$	$1, 1$

$x =$ one million

Kohlberg and Mertens (1986) feel that for the game above with $x = 3$, noncooperative game theory has nothing to offer that will eliminate the equilibrium $\langle 1, 1 \rangle$, and that such considerations should fall under the relatively restricted domain of cooperative game theory. However, at least one implication we might draw from the recent interest in criteria that admit correlated behavior of various sorts (Aumann 1987, Kreps and Ramey 1987) is that traditional views of "coordinative" behavior may not be so obviously true, even if they do turn out to be true in the end. And, if we allow contexts to determine the appropriateness of different solution criteria for the same game, as Kreps has recommended, then there seems little doubt that there is a place for solution concepts that explicitly admit both conflictual and coordinative aspects of the game.

As a first and obvious move toward this we will adopt the mixed "Pareto-Nash" criterion we defined above. Note that the game we have defined above is a pure coordination game (of partial information) and in such games the set of Pareto-dominant strategies is a subset of the set of Nash equilibria so that there is no conflict between the two solution concepts considered independently. But we will consider more general mixed-motive games below and we will use the same criterion for these games as well. The Pareto-Nash criterion is admittedly a rather simple concept and is unlikely to have much force. But it should be seen as a first step.

When we apply the Pareto criterion to the Nash equilibrium set $\{N_1, N_2\}$ we find that N_2 gets eliminated, as required. The expected payoff from N_1 to both players is $.9(10) + .1(7) = 9.7$. The expected payoff to both players from N_2 is $.9(7) + .1(10) = 7.3$. This implies that N_1 Pareto-dominates N_2 and that both players can with certainty choose N_1. Since s is factual, this results in $\mathcal{A}$ saying φ and in $\mathcal{B}$ choosing p rather than q.

This completes our discussion of how the game $LG(\varphi)$ is solved. We will call a strategy that satisfies this solution concept a Pareto-Nash equilibrium. N_1 turns out to be the unique Pareto-Nash equilibrium of $LG(\varphi)$ and so its value $v[LG(\varphi)]$ is 10, as we had asserted above.

Note that if we assume equal probabilities instead of skewed probabilities ("A comet appears every ten years") we are unable to eliminate the second solution N_2 and this squares with our intuition as well. In this case the optimal solution would seem to be to spell out the content literally by using ψ_1 as φ remains ambiguous. This is interesting because it shows us how to justify the use of a more elaborate expression to avoid an ineliminable ambiguity. Also, if we have skewed probabilities as above, but s' is factual rather than s, then again the optimal strategy is to spell things out by using ψ_2 instead of ψ.[8]

How do we define the value of a game that has multiple equilibria? In the usual way, as the expected value of the set of multiple values. However, it is unclear what distribution we should use in evaluating expected values. We will assume that, in the absence of any further information, each equilibrium strategy is equally likely. In the case of the comet we considered above, where s and s' have the same likelihood of occurrence, $\mathcal{A}$ should assign equal probabilities to both solutions in the absence of any information about a preference that $\mathcal{B}$ might have for one or the other. Thus, if $\mathcal{B}$ plays N_1 they get 10 and if he plays N_2 they get -10, and the expected value of this set of two values with

---

The various conflictual solution concepts that have been investigated show much sophistication in exploiting the conflictual elements in games. There does not seem any a priori reason to limit the possibilities for sophisticated "cooperative" or coordinative behavior, as long as such behavior cannot be subverted by conflictual behavior, of course.

It is worth pointing out explicitly that the entire discussion above is based on three imprecise but suggestive premises. The first is an intuitive notion of the degree of conflict and coordination in a game. The second is an extremely vague notion of the possibility of separating the conflictual and coordinative aspects of a game. And the third is the identification of the motivations underlying most existing solution concepts with the conflictual aspects of games. It is unclear whether any of these premises would hold up under more rigorous scrutiny. But we must leave our discussion of these issues here and return to our main story.

[8]See footnote 2 in this chapter.

respect to a uniform distribution is just 0. This is the value that $\mathcal{A}$ should consider in making her optimal decision in the global game.

We need to make certain that every game $LG(\psi)$ that $\mathcal{A}$ might consider does in fact have a value. This is guaranteed to us by a theorem of Nash's (1951) (and its extension by Harsanyi 1967 to the existence of Bayesian-Nash equilibria). Every game has at least one Nash equilibrium in the larger space of mixed strategies. In fact, it is easy to show that every game of pure coordination (games in which players have identical payoff functions) has an equilibrium in pure strategies. In either case, this guarantees in turn that every SDM has a solution. (Actually, the step to the existence of a solution for every SDM isn't quite so immediate. It requires a consistency condition between the local and global games to be satisfied. We will state this condition in the next chapter.)

This completes our analysis of why $\mathcal{A}$ chooses to say φ in the utterance situation u, and correspondingly of how $\mathcal{B}$ comes to choose the right interpretation p in the interpretive situation i. But our model, the SDM, is not really firmly grounded in the discourse situation as yet. We need to show exactly where this game of partial information is located, whether it is in the "minds" of the agents concerned or whether it is in the ambient circumstances that make up the discourse situation, or both or neither. Situating the SDM will give us a complete model of the communicative transfer between $\mathcal{A}$ and $\mathcal{B}$.

We also need to discuss the many assumptions we have made, both the CICM assumptions and a few other assumptions we made implicitly along the way. This will suggest some possible refinements of our analysis, and we will develop one of these briefly.

Also, so far we have been using an intuitive notion of communication. Once we have situated the SDM and discussed the assumptions and some extensions of our model, it will be possible for us to suggest how this notion can be made rigorous in terms of our model.

We turn first to situating the SDM.

2.4 Games and Situations

We started our analysis of the strategic inference with a discourse situation d from which we extracted an utterance situation u and an interpretive situation i. We can extract two more situations from each of u and i. From u we extract the choice situation c_u and the "production" situation p_u. The choice situation is the situation in which $\mathcal{A}$ considers her choice structure and p_u is the situation in which she issues or produces her optimal choice. We have two similar situations for $\mathcal{B}$, a choice situation c_i in which he considers his choice structure, and an interpretation situation i_i in which he picks the optimal interpretation. Both c_i and i_i are parts of i.

A little situation theory is called for at this point. We will treat all situations as sets of (located) states of affairs. A state of affairs is an $(n + 2)$-tuple $\langle\!\langle R_n\,;\, x_1, \ldots, x_n\,;\, i\,\rangle\!\rangle$ where R_n is an n-place relation, $\{x_1, \ldots, x_n\}$ is its set of arguments, and the i is a polarity which can be either 1 or 0. If i is 1, the state of affairs presents the possible fact that the relation R_n holds of $\langle x_1, \ldots, x_n\rangle$. If i is zero, it presents the opposite possibility, that the relation does not hold of the individuals in question. We will also require that all states of affairs be located in some (connected) space-time region l.

For example, a possible situation based on our example above might be $a = \{\langle\!\langle l\,;\, saying\,;\, \mathcal{A}, \varphi, \mathcal{B}\,;\, 1\,\rangle\!\rangle\}$, where l might be, say, Riverside Park in New York in 1987. This is a situation in which we have $\mathcal{A}$ saying φ to $\mathcal{B}$ at l. If the situation describes that slice of the world correctly, we would say that a is factual and that the single state of affairs in a is a fact. In general, of course, situations will contain many states of affairs.

One situation is a part of another or is contained in another when it is a subset of the other. For example, the situation a above would be a part of the production situation p_u. Also, the discourse situation d has as parts u and i, which in turn have the parts c_u, p_u and c_i, i_i respectively. We will in fact define u as the union of its two subsets above, as we will i. The discourse situation d will in our particular example be taken as the union of u and i. In general, however, it will contain a "sequence" of utterance, (reception), and interpretive situations. More generally yet, it will contain a series of utterances and interpretations intertwined with other actions.

We need to spell out then exactly what the two choice situations contain. $\mathcal{A}$'s choice situation c_u contains s (from $LG(\varphi)$) as a subsituation. We had said earlier that s contains the fact that $\mathcal{A}$ intends to convey p. The situation c_u also contains all the constraints that describe the SDM. For example, it contains the constraint that if $\mathcal{A}$ says φ $\mathcal{B}$ will construct $LG(\varphi)$ in c_i. Another constraint is that if $\mathcal{A}$ says φ the situation t will be factual (and a subsituation of c_i). The entire structure of the SDM, the global game and all the local games, are thus embedded in c_u.

$\mathcal{B}$'s choice situation is similar. It contains t as a part though $\mathcal{B}$ does not know that t is a part of c_i. It also contains the constraints that capture the local game $LG(\varphi)$. Note that other situations like e or t' never become factual and so never become direct parts of c_i. They enter into the various constraints that make up the SDM and so enter into c_u and c_i only indirectly (as "constituents").

Two interesting facts emerge by situating the SDM in this way. The first is that one aspect of the nonwellfoundedness of SDM's (and games in general) becomes explicit. For example, c_u and c_i both contain some of the same constraints. Common knowledge of these constraints, which is an additional constraint in both c_u and c_i, then makes both situations jointly nonwellfounded. (See Barwise 1989a.)

The second point of interest is that situating the two choice structures ($\mathcal{A}$'s and $\mathcal{B}$'s) in two separate situations makes it possible to construct in a natural way more general strategic interactions than the ones traditionally modeled in game theory. This more general kind of interaction becomes crucial when we want to define communicative situations and distinguish them from noncommunicative transfers of information. Essentially, each choice situation contains a model of the interaction between $\mathcal{A}$ and $\mathcal{B}$. These models may or may not be the same and may or may not be common knowledge. For example, $\mathcal{A}$ and $\mathcal{B}$ might construct different local games $LG(\varphi)$, or $LG(\varphi)$ may not be common knowledge. Such situations are not games even though they are interactive choice situations. It is difficult to give any sort of general description of such models because such situations are of many different types. They also raise deep and interesting questions about the nature and meaning of solution concepts. It is important to mention that though they are difficult to model such situations are not uncommon. We will look at a simple instance of such a situation when we consider communicative and noncommunicative transfers of information.

Our CICM assumptions also describe constraints and these are also situated. We said above in fact that the Communication and Information Assumptions are located in the background B which is a large situation that contains d and much else. We have said that these background assumptions are common knowledge; we can assume further that they are not part of their so-called "activated" common knowledge, in that agents do not need to consider them explicitly each time they communicate. The Circumstantial Assumptions are constraints in c_u and c_i.

This completes our situation of the SDM. We can see that many of the constraints exist both in the ambient circumstances as well as in the store of knowledge of the agents. We have avoided a more detailed account of this situation. This would involve building in the insights currently being developed by Barwise and Perry (see, for example, Perry 1986b). But this limited embedding of the SDM suffices for our purposes, and has some very interesting consequences for our conception of communication that we will spell out below.

We now have a complete model of the communicative transfer of p from $\mathcal{A}$ to $\mathcal{B}$, relative to our assumptions. Our next step is to look at some aspects of these assumptions more closely.

2.5   The Assumptions

Communication is an involved process and thus involves a number of assumptions! We collected most of these under the banner "CICM Assumptions." In this section we will comment on some of these in more detail.

Consider the second Communication Assumption that agents prefer more relevant information to less (ceteris paribus), in the absence of indications to the contrary. There are two features about this assumption that require comment. First, it is consonant with similar assumptions about various market commodities that are made in economics. It is generally assumed that more of a good is preferred to less. This is reflected in the assumption of concave utility functions (concave in commodity space). However, (like money), information is a peculiar second-order type of thing. Though it may be preferred for its own sake, it is typically preferred because it facilitates the satisfaction of other ("first-order") goals.[9] This distinction is reflected in the parallel distinction made in statistical decision theory between information-gathering acts or *experiments* and utility-generating acts or *terminal acts* (Arrow 1974). It should therefore be derivable from these first-order goals. This fact is reflected in the second feature we wish to note, the assumption that it is relevant information that is preferred. We will suggest later how the notion of relevance might be made more precise by bringing in the idea of the value of information. This idea directly involves goals and payoffs and so provides additional confirmation of our point about the derivability of this assumption from more basic assumptions.

We also assumed that rational agents minimize effort or cost. The costs associated with a communicative transfer are of various kinds, including costs of processing, memory, and transmission. In the model we constructed we implicitly assumed that these costs were shared (more or less) equally. This is unlikely to be true in general, and a more detailed consideration of costs would make a more accurate allocation possible. This is something we will not pursue here, however. As we stated above, in the kinds of situations we're considering, costs are relatively

---

[9] In fact, money may be viewed as a device for summarizing (or perhaps, obviating the need for) a wide range of economy-wide information!

small, so that the *SDM* is unlikely to be too sensitive to variations in cost allocations.

Our fourth Communication Assumption of cooperation also makes this sharing of costs a reasonable approximation to adopt, especially for the kinds of situations we are looking at. This assumption of cooperation derives essentially from Grice (1975). It is possible to view this crucial assumption as itself a necessary outcome of the demands of rational interaction, however different and potentially conflictual the "ultimate" ends of individuals might be. Arrow (1974) cites some reasons for such a possibility in the context of collective action generally. Essentially, collective action (i.e. social "institutions") can extend the domain of individual rationality in a number of ways.[10] Strawson's (1986) remark that the cooperative assumption is "a precondition of the possibility of the social institution of language" might be seen in this light. Arrow's nuanced observations on the "invisible" institutions of ethics and morality as an important means for securing the mutual benefits of collective action make relatively weaker claims for the role and status of cooperation. We will leave it at that with two further comments. First, a precise statement of this assumption presupposes a calculus of hierarchies of goals and preferences. Second, the remarks above touch upon the purely functional or instrumental aspect of these difficult issues.

Our last two assumptions in this set have to do with the language used by the speaker and addressee. The first of these states that A and B share a language $\mathcal{L}$. This is admittedly a little vague, but we have left it so intentionally. It is in fact possible to develop an independent game-theoretic account of what it is to share a language. Lewis (1975) gives an outline of one such account. Assuming that the notion of sharing a language can be made precise isn't enough to justify our assumption, however. In fact, the assumption that they share an entire language is a strong one and is not strictly necessary for the communication to occur. We will assume it, however, to keep things simple. In general, agents may share (partially) more than one language (or communication system, more generally). This possibility raises two questions. One is the question of the optimal choice of language for a particular communication, and the other is the deciphering (by the addressee) of what language or code is being used. We will make the simplifying assumption here that A and B share just one language $\mathcal{L}$.

---

[10] One way in which this can happen is through the need for some sufficiently complex social system to mediate the competition for scarce resources; a second is through the possible gains of cooperation, as a result of the nonuniform distribution of capacities and talents in a group, and the nonuniform development of these capacities that occurs as a result of collaborative specialization.

The next assumption is that $\mathfrak{L}$ is a sufficiently expressive language. This turns out to be an important assumption in our account of how communication takes place. If it is impossible to express a proposition in some alternative way, then the information communicable via $\mathfrak{L}$ is limited in important ways. It should be clear from our construction above where this assumption enters the model. (See Figures 2.3 and 2.4.) This assumption can be made precise in a number of different ways. We will indicate some of the important alternatives. First, we might assume that every proposition can be expressed minimally. (This is what we did in fact assume.) However, this assumption is not strictly necessary. If there is no way to express a proposition minimally, we could do either of two things. One is to consider sentences that express only a proper part of this proposition minimally. This would result in a reduced payoff. In our example, ψ_1 and ψ_2 led to lower payoffs as a result of higher costs. In general, both higher costs and lower amounts of information may reduce payoffs. Alternatively, we could consider a slightly more complex *SDM*, one in which the minimal content of these alternative expressions would be different from the intended contents, as is the case with φ. As with the other assumptions we will stick to the simpler versions of this assumption as well.

Finally, all these assumptions need to be common knowledge between $\mathcal{A}$ and $\mathcal{B}$. We will see the crucial importance of this in the section below on communication. All these assumptions are located in the background situation B. The import of this is simply that agents can be assumed to obey them in any discourse situation we might consider, since any d will always be a part of B. Again, strictly speaking, some of our considerations above relating to the detailed nature of the payoff function clearly belong in the discourse situation rather than in B. That is, they ought to be part of the Circumstantial Assumptions rather than part of the Communication Assumptions. But, since they will be true of the full range of discourse situations we will consider, we will simply relegate them to the background, and leave it at that for now.

The Circumstantial Assumptions are, as the name suggests, assumptions that vary with the (relatively variable) discourse circumstances, that is, with d. In the example we considered, the discourse information available to $\mathcal{A}$ and $\mathcal{B}$ was kept to a minimum. In larger discourse situations, (ones with more u situations and i situations, and other acts), a lot more information is generally available to both agents. In particular, it is possible for $\mathcal{B}$ to have some (shared) information about $\mathcal{A}$'s initial choice set. This would allow for interesting variations in the game-theoretic structure we've constructed. In this dissertation, however, we will stick to simpler games of the type above.

A crucial assumption we made in our analysis is that A and B have available to them shared knowledge of what we've called the minimal content of φ in d, namely the proposition $p \lor q$. We have also maintained that every utterance has a minimal content, which will in general be different from the intended or communicated content. One can think (loosely) of the minimal content as similar to the literal content. For certain strategic inferences (implicatures) the minimal content is the same as the literal content. Thus, the notion of a minimal content is a generalization of the notion of a literal content. It is possible to develop a simultaneous equation model that incorporates all the strategic inferences involved in understanding an utterance. In such a model, the intended content would be given directly as the solution of the relevant system of equations. Intermediate contents like minimal contents would then be solutions to proper subsets of the full set of equations. What we are doing is abstracting from the larger set of equations and studying just one strategic inference, assuming that we are given the minimal content or solution to the remaining equations that we have abstracted from.

We also made some assumptions of convenience along the way. One such assumption was that both agents use the same sentences ψ_1 and ψ_2 in the local games $LG(\varphi)$ they construct. It is easy to see that this assumption is not really necessary. All we need is (common knowledge of the fact) that there is at least one sentence with the relevant properties in the language $\mathfrak{L}$. This is, of course, guaranteed by the expressiveness of $\mathfrak{L}$. A and B do not even need to have any particular sentence in mind, as long as they know such a sentence is available. Secondly, the payoff functions that A and B use don't need to be identical, as long as each is a positive linear transformation of the other. Thirdly, the particular numerical probabilities we assigned don't matter, and they can even be different for the two players as long as one is greater than the other.

There were two fundamental assumptions we made implicitly. The first is the assumption that B's interpretive act is publicly observable. Interpretive acts are obviously unobservable, let alone being publicly so. This implies that the payoffs A and B receive at the end of the game are not publicly observable. This is true of many discourse situations. Often, it will be unclear to the agents involved if the communication was successful or not. In an ongoing discourse, the particular interpretation B chose may be inferable from subsequent actions by B. This suggests some interesting modifications of the model we've developed above. Just as the contents of utterances are not immediately given, so are the contents of interpretive acts. Once again, however, we will not pursue these possibilities in this dissertation.

The second basic assumption we made implicitly is in our model of the communicative process as an utterance situation followed by an interpretive situation. This assumption calls for a detailed consideration.

2.6 Games and Attitudes

In the strategic discourse model we set up above we had B performing the act of interpreting A's utterance. A utters a sentence φ and B interprets it. And the structure that enables them to get p across turns out to be a game of partial information of the kind we constructed above.

A complete joint act of communication involves the performance of many separate acts by both speaker and addressee. Austin (1961/1979) classified the various speech acts performed by a speaker into locutionary, illocutionary, and perlocutionary acts. On the addressee's side, the acts performed as part of a communicative act may be classified (roughly) into acts of perception or reception (of the utterance), interpretive acts (or acts of "understanding" or "securing uptake"), and "responsive" acts (or acts that are appropriate responses to the message). In our model we implicitly abstracted from the illocutionary act performed by A in saying φ, namely the act of informing B. B cannot be said to have understood A's utterance unless he also understands this further aspect of A's utterance, called its (illocutionary) force. That is, B's interpretive act should involve not just figuring out the content of φ in d but also its force. If we assume that A and B are located in Riverside Park in New York, it is easy to imagine somewhat different Circumstantial Assumptions that make the same utterance a warning.

Typically, the point of performing an illocutionary act in addition to the locutionary act of saying something is to get the addressee to do something, to influence his actions, beliefs, or other attitudes. That is, the speaker will want the addressee not simply to interpret her utterance but to perform some further action based on this interpretation. In our example, A will want B to accept the proposition p, that is to come to believe p. In general, B has the choice of either accepting or rejecting the information that A conveys to him. (More generally, he can accept it probabilistically.) If A had instead said to B, "Leave the room," A would have, in the appropriate circumstances, performed the (illocutionary) act of requesting B to leave the room, and intended that B leave the room, not simply interpret her utterance. And B would have had the option of complying with the request or disregarding it.

How does B know what kind of action he is to perform? He needs to identify the (illocutionary) force of the utterance in addition to its content. And once he has done this, he has to decide whether to perform the relevant action intended by $\mathcal{A}$ or not.

This requires two modifications of the *SDM* we considered above. Now we have $\mathcal{B}$ performing two actions after hearing (receiving) $\mathcal{A}$'s utterance. The first action is interpreting the utterance (i.e. identifying its force and content) and the second is accepting or rejecting it. We will continue to abstract from the first problem of identifying the force, and consider the second action, assuming that the force is given (in much the same way as we assumed that the minimal content was given). This leads to the game in Figure 2.8.

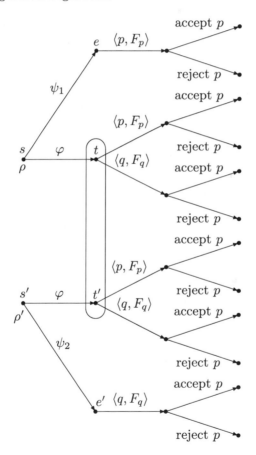

FIGURE 2.8 Games with Attitudes

The notation F_p stands in general for the force with which a proposition has to be interpreted. In the tree above, given our Circumstantial Assumptions, F_p stands for the fact that $\mathcal{A}$ is simply conveying the information p to $\mathcal{B}$. The tuple $\langle p, F_p \rangle$ is the full information communicated.

We have deliberately not put in payoffs at the terminal situations. Our purpose here is simply to point out the kind of game that we get when we consider a more complete model of communication. We would need additional assumptions to fill in appropriate payoff functions. $\mathcal{B}$ may or may not be predisposed to accepting or rejecting $\mathcal{A}$'s information (perhaps as a result of his own experiences in NYC). And this predilection of $\mathcal{B}$'s may or may not be common knowledge. This situation makes possible a divergence of interests between speaker and addressee. $\mathcal{A}$'s goal is presumably to get $\mathcal{B}$ to believe a proposition with the least possible effort on her part. But $\mathcal{B}$ may need more evidence than just a bald assertion of a fact if he's going to believe it. That is, the least cost sentence may not be the one that is optimal. Earlier, we had a game of pure coordination, one in which both players had identical payoffs. Now we get a game in which the payoff functions for each player may be quite different from each other.

Note that the communicative act itself does not include the particular intended response (accepting a proposition or leaving a room) as a constituent act. The communicative act goes through once $\mathcal{B}$ interprets $\mathcal{A}$'s utterance correctly. But, in general, it will be necessary for $\mathcal{B}$ (and $\mathcal{A}$) to explicitly consider the possible actions $\mathcal{B}$ might respond with, the corresponding payoff functions, and their shared knowledge of this larger structure in order to communicate successfully.

This kind of (local) game turns out to be almost identical to what have been called "signaling games" in the information economics literature (see Kreps 1987 for a definition and a bibliography). The only difference lies in the larger global structure in which these local games are embedded (and therefore, also in the interpretation of local games). We call the kinds of games we've constructed games of partial information (instead of incomplete information) to note this crucial difference. One can see games of incomplete information as special instances of games of partial information, instances in which player $\mathcal{A}$'s (range of possible) choice sets are fully and publicly known before the game starts. A strategic discourse model might then be described as a signaling game of partial information.

We should point out that this analysis does not apply to all communicative acts. As Strawson (1964) has emphasized, there is a whole "continuum" of communicative acts ranging from "essentially" conventional to "essentially" nonconventional. Our example is an instance of a nonconventional communicative act. Conventional acts (redoubling at bridge, for example) are acts whose intended responses are secured simply by their being performed in the right circumstances, including among other things the fact that the relevant convention be common knowledge between speaker and addressee(s). But what is common to all communicative acts is that both the content and the force of the utterance be understood for successful communication. In some cases this will involve a consideration of addressee response, in others it will not.

It is thus useful to have both types of models, those of pure coordination and those with possible conflict, when we look at various types of communication. Also, the second type of model includes the first type, and when there is no special information about the prior acceptability or otherwise of a proposition to the addressee, the second model is essentially equivalent to the first.

We turn now to an account of communication.

2.7 Situated Communication

We will assume a familiarity with the Gricean approach to meaning in this section. This includes not only Grice's (1957, 1969, 1968) own accounts but also its various modifications, especially those proposed by Strawson (1964), Schiffer (1972), and Searle (1983). We will indicate how the central insights of this approach can be accommodated in a natural way in our account of situated communication, that is, within the model-theoretic perspective of situation theory and the game-and-situation-theoretic perspective of the *SDM*.

The many complexities of the problem (e.g. Grice or Schiffer) as well as the incomplete development of the *SDM* precludes anything like a complete account of communication. Our strategy will be to stick to the example above and educe, more or less informally, the essential features of such an account.

Roughly, there are three sorts of constraints that are necessary and sufficient for communication. The first (and relatively obvious, when stated so vaguely) constraint is that communication be a genuinely interactive process. The second constraint, which is the crucial one, is that certain aspects of this interaction be common knowledge (or at least mutually believed). The third and final constraint is that this shared interaction be situated (which is to say, as we will see, that it be efficient in a certain way).

It should be clear from our detailed development of the example how the *SDM* provides a model of a "genuinely" interactive process. Essentially, the interaction must be strategic, in the precise sense given to this concept by game theory and by the *SDM*.

It is the role of common knowledge that requires scrutiny, and we will see why through a well-known counterexample by Strawson (1964). We will consider Schiffer's more complete version of Strawson's example. Suppose A wants B to think that the house he is thinking of buying is rat-infested. A decides to bring about this belief in B by letting loose a rat in the house. She knows that B is watching her and knows that B believes that A is unaware that B is watching her. A intends B to infer, wrongly, from the fact that she let the rat loose that she did so with the intention that B should see the rat, take the rat as "natural" evidence, and infer therefrom that the house is rat-infested. A further intends B to realize that the presence of the rat cannot be taken as genuine evidence; but A knows that B will think that A would not so contrive to get B to believe the house is rat-infested unless A had good reasons for thinking it was, and so intends B to infer that the house is rat-infested from the fact that A is letting the rat loose with the intention of getting B to believe that the house is rat-infested.

It should be clear, intuitively, that this is not a case of communication (or even of attempted communication). There is, however, a (noncommunicative) transfer or flow of information from A to B and we can construct a strategic discourse model for this flow in much the same way as we did for the communicative transfer. This is made significantly easier by our situation of A's and B's choice structures in two distinct situations, u and i. This is a discourse situation in which A and B have different models of their interaction.

Consider the two trees T_1 and T_2, in Figures 2.9 and 2.10 respectively, where p stands for the proposition that the house is rat-infested and q is its negation.

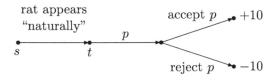

FIGURE 2.9 Partial Information T_1

T_1 represents the proposition that a rat appears "naturally" in the house, B interprets this situation as a sign that the house is rat-infested and has a choice of accepting or rejecting this proposition p. The payoffs are as they are because it would be irrational not to accept such natural evidence as indicating p. T_1 is not common knowledge (or mutual belief) of course. According to the story, $\mathcal{B}$ believes that $\mathcal{A}$ believes that $\mathcal{B}$ believes the proposition represented by T_1.

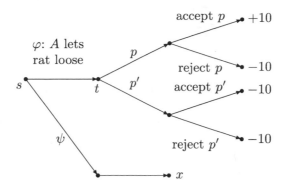

FIGURE 2.10 Partial Information T_2

T_2 is incompletely specified. It represents two sets of choices, one for $\mathcal{A}$ and one for $\mathcal{B}$. $\mathcal{A}$ can choose to "utter" φ, which is to let the rat loose. Or $\mathcal{A}$ can choose another action ψ. It is not obvious what other action(s) $\mathcal{A}$ might consider. One possibility is for $\mathcal{A}$ not to do anything, in which case there is nothing for $\mathcal{B}$ to interpret and the payoff x is 0. Another possibility is for $\mathcal{A}$ to *tell* $\mathcal{B}$ that the house is rat-infested. Schiffer's story compels us to assume that for some (unspecified) reason or other, this communicative action is relatively inefficient. That is, better payoffs are available if $\mathcal{A}$ chooses φ instead of an appropriate linguistic ψ. We need not concern ourselves with the nature of these possibilities as long as we assume that any other ψ yields a payoff x that is less than at least one payoff resulting from φ. If $\mathcal{A}$ chooses φ $\mathcal{B}$ can infer either p or its negation q, and once again he has the choice of accepting or rejecting either proposition.

The information in the story that determines the payoffs here should be located in the initial situation s. $\mathcal{A}$'s intention here is that $\mathcal{B}$ infer p (rather than q) by wrongly taking the rat's presence as natural evidence, that is, by assuming T_1 to be the case rather than T_2. If this were all, $\mathcal{B}$ should be inclined to reject rather than accept p. But it is further assumed that $\mathcal{A}$ knows that $\mathcal{B}$ knows that $\mathcal{A}$ would not expend such efforts without good reason, hence that knowledge of $\mathcal{A}$'s intention rather than the actual presence of the rat should be $\mathcal{B}$'s reason for accepting p. This knowledge of $\mathcal{B}$'s is what determines the payoffs. Accepting p has a high (relative) payoff of 10 and rejecting it has a low payoff of -10. Interpreting the action as conveying q has a low payoff in both cases because the flow is misinformational, that is, B would be wrongly interpreting A as conveying q.

T_2 is also not common knowledge. B believes the proposition represented by T_2 to be true. B knows that the proposition expressed by T_1 is false but thinks that A believes that B believes it to be true. Further, B also believes that A does not know that B believes T_2 to be true. These three beliefs, all located in t, provide a model of B's choice situation c_i. We will call B's choice structure SDM_B. Note that SDM_B contains two distinct trees, with a more or less complex connection between them.

A knows all three of B's beliefs. This makes the proposition represented by T_2 false as well because A's true intention is not correctly represented. A's true intention is that B have the three beliefs above and reason as above to infer and accept p. Thus, A's choice structure, which we will call SDM_A, contains the same two trees T_1 and T_2, and a third tree T_3 with the same structure as T_2 but with the initial situation containing A's true intention rather than the false intention above.

The SDM for this flow of information is then simply the pair $\langle SDM_A, SDM_B \rangle$, SDM_A being situated in u and SDM_B in i. The first choice structure is A's model of the strategic interaction, the second is B's. Note that there is no common knowledge of any choice structure. This SDM is also a new type of interactive choice situation that has not been studied before. It is not a game, not even of partial information, because the common knowledge requirement is not satisfied. We will call such more general situations strategic interactions. Strategic interactions will be games only when the common knowledge condition is fulfilled. Every discourse situation can, in principle, be modeled as a strategic interaction by an SDM.

Intuitively, it is clear that the rational choice for A is to do φ and for B to accept p. Thus, p flows from A to B even though the transfer is not a communicative one. We will not attempt to define a formal solution concept for this SDM. When we give up the assumption of common knowledge the strategic interaction becomes quite complex and the first task would be to define the class of these more general choice structures. They range roughly from one extreme in which each agent has minimal knowledge of the other agent's model (this is like the single-person choice model assumed in the theory of competitive equilibrium in economics) to the other extreme of full common knowledge (assumed in game theory).

Schiffer in particular has devised a number of similar examples of increasing complexity to argue convincingly that nothing short of common knowledge of the strategic interaction between A and B is adequate for communication. The key point, as Strawson has pointed out, is that there must not be any latent intentions, as in T_3 above. Clark and Marshall (1981) make a similar point in a somewhat different context. Such considerations account for our second constraint on communication.

Our last constraint is that communication be situated. We have already indicated how *SDM*s are situated. In the Gricean approach we are led inexorably (by the considerations cited above) to postulate intentions of increasing complexity. Even in the original definition proposed by Grice a quite complex intention (made up of three subintentions) is required. This so-called M-intention is needed to ensure that the flow of information occurs in the right way and for the right reasons. In the Gricean approach agents and their interactions are not assumed to be situated with the result that all the "work" has to be done by the cognitive states of agents.

As Barwise (1989c) and Perry (1986a) have pointed out, taking the situatedness of information flows seriously relieves the agents from considering all the relevant aspects of the embedding circumstances. Just as, to take Perry's example, an agent does not need to have beliefs about the ambient gravitational force when reaching for a glass of water (or even about the distance between the agent and the glass), so communicating agents do not need to have all the complex intentions apparently required of communication. The structure of the embedding circumstances, that is, the *SDM*, does much of the work. The only intention required of A is the intention to convey a proposition, or if we include a consideration of addressee response, then to evoke a certain type of response by conveying a certain proposition. We will not argue the case in detail here, but it should be easy to see that the *SDM* does in fact satisfy the conditions fulfilled by all the Gricean intentions.

Just as the noncircumstantial account of beliefs overburdens the belief-forming capacities of agents so the unsituated Gricean approach overburdens the intention-forming capacities of agents. As Perry has pointed out, a circumstantial account does not preclude the possibility of an agent having additional and unnecessary beliefs, and similarly, agents are certainly free to have M-intentions should they so prefer. But, situated communication is more efficient than unsituated communication and rational agents will naturally exploit their ambient circumstances optimally. Thus, strictly speaking, situated communication is not an additional necessary condition for communication but is a consequence of the rationality of agents. However, once we take the finiteness of agents seriously, exploiting the situatedness of communication may be the only way (rather than the simply the most efficient way) of effecting certain transfers of information. It is with this in mind that we include it as an independent necessary constraint.

We can now indicate what a definition of communication that incorporates all three constraints would look like. Note that every *SDM* is a strategic interaction. We will assume further that every discourse situation and background pair $\langle d, B \rangle$ "induces" an *SDM*.

We will say that an agent $\mathcal{A}$ communicates something to another agent $\mathcal{B}$ by producing φ in discourse situation d and background B if and only if the *SDM* induced by $\langle d, B \rangle$ is a (situated) game of partial information. What $\mathcal{A}$ communicates to $\mathcal{B}$ will be given by the (Pareto-Nash) equilibrium of the *SDM*.

The concept of nonnatural meaning can now be defined as attempted communication. That is, $\mathcal{A}$ nonnaturally means something (by producing φ) if $\mathcal{A}$ attempts to communicate something to some $\mathcal{B}$ by producing φ (in some d and B). There are other problems with the Gricean account that our situated game-theoretic account must also solve, but our (simple) intention here is merely to indicate what such an account must look like, rather than to give a full-fledged formal definition.

Communication is an example of a joint or collective act. Our analysis here suggests that other joint acts might also be analyzed in similar ways, as situated games.

This concludes our justification of the claim made at the beginning of this chapter that if the CICM assumptions (as well as the Unspecified Assumptions) are satisfied $\mathcal{A}$ will succeed in communicating p to $\mathcal{B}$.

2.8   Conclusion

We have examined one strategic inference in detail in this chapter and have given an informal account of how it works. In doing so, we have had to develop some new ideas. The key ones are the concepts of situated games of partial information, (situated) strategic interactions, and situated communication. Our model, the *SDM*, illustrates all these concepts.

In the next chapter we give a formal definition of a subclass of (communicative) *SDM*s. Once we have this, we can define a mapping from the ordered pair $\langle d, B \rangle$ to the set of communicated contents $\mathcal{C}$. If we call this mapping $\mathfrak{SDM}$, we can write this as $\mathfrak{SDM}(d, B) = \mathcal{C}$. We could make the sentence (or action) in d explicit and also write $\mathfrak{SDM}(\varphi, d, B) = \mathcal{C}$. In our example above, we would have $\mathfrak{SDM}(\varphi, d, B) = \{p\}$.

The *SDM* can thus be viewed as a (partial) account of the fundamental equation of situation semantics (and, indeed, of semantics generally) that links (situated) utterances with contents.

3

Situations, Games, and the Strategic Discourse Model

3.1 Introduction

In this chapter, we will give a formal model of some of the ideas we discussed in Chapter 2. Situation theory, developed by Barwise and Perry, provides a rich framework for a general theory of information. Choice and game theory provide a rich framework for studying the actions and interactions of rational agents. In part, this dissertation is concerned to bring these two frameworks together to develop the tools required to study problems of communication and more general transfers of information among rational agents.

Our central task in this chapter will be to show how games can be constructed from situations, not unlike the way in which numbers can be constructed from sets. We will do this for a limited class of games.

Traditionally, games are defined directly. Kreps and Wilson (1982) provide a formulation that is now quite standard. We will use their formulation of a game of incomplete information as a tuple of various sets as the approximate goal of our construction. This goal is approximate because the game we construct is what we have called a game of partial information and is in certain important respects different from a game of incomplete information. Our situation-theoretic construction is meant to serve three purposes. The first is simply to provide an illustration of the richness of situation theory as a foundational theory. The second is to provide a framework for the concept of information. The third purpose is one we mentioned in Chapter 2. Constructing games from situations allows one a finer-grained universe of objects that facilitates a consideration of more general choice-theoretic structures as well as some important distinctions in a natural way. Though we do not pursue these more general strategic interactions here, our more limited construction will suggest how such a project might be attempted.

We will not attempt anything like a complete formal construction with some minimal set of primitive objects and conditions on these objects. A game is a relatively complex object and requires a host of simpler objects for its construction. All these would themselves need to be defined situation-theoretically on the way to constructing a game. We will use a small part of the version of situation theory in *Situations and Attitudes* and in *The Liar* and also a few other objects directly.

A complete construction would in any case be a difficult task given the many complexities of strategic interactions. Our effort here is to show that it can be carried out and that it is a useful thing to do, quite apart from its intrinsic mathematical interest.

3.2   Games

Kreps and Wilson (1982) define a game of incomplete information as a tuple $\langle T, \prec; ACT, \alpha; N, \eta; \rho; H; v \rangle$. T is a set of nodes and $\prec$ is a partial ordering on T that makes the pair $\langle T, \prec \rangle$ a tree (more precisely an arborescence, that is, a tree with more than one initial node). ACT is a set of actions and α is a function that maps every noninitial node of $\langle T, \prec \rangle$ into some action in ACT. Intuitively, this is intended to be the action that leads to this node. N is a set of agents (or players) and η is a mapping from the set of nonterminal nodes onto N. Intuitively, η establishes whose turn it is to act. ρ is a vector of probabilities on the set of initial nodes. This much of the tuple gives us, under the above interpretation, a tree with decision nodes connected by actions and with an agent identified for each decision node. H is a partition on T that consists of subpartitions, one for each player. It is meant to capture the information sets of each agent, the sets of decision nodes of an agent that cannot be distinguished by the agent. Accordingly, each agent's subpartition is a collection of those sets of nodes that are its information sets. Finally, v is the payoff function, a mapping from the terminal nodes into the set $\Re$ of real numbers. This is an informal description of the tuple we will be constructing (approximately) and the reader is referred to Kreps and Wilson's paper for the formal definitions.

It is clear from our discussion of Chapter 2 that the set of nodes T can be treated as a set of situations. This is the key idea of our construction. We will first introduce the situation theory we need and then describe the other objects we will need for our construction.

3.3   Situations

A1. Situation Theory

We will assume as given a set A of individuals and a set R of properties and relations. From these, we can construct tuples called states of affairs $\langle\!\langle R_n, a_1, \ldots, a_n \, ; \, i \rangle\!\rangle$ where i can be 1 or 0. (States of affairs typically have an additional parameter, a space-time location. We will ignore this here because we do not really need it for our construction.) The set of states of affairs will be denoted by SOA. Situations are constructed as sets of states of affairs, and the set of situations will be denoted by SIT. And propositions are built up as special sets of situations, the set of propositions being called $PROP$. This much gives us our basic building blocks. Note that we are not using all the situation theory developed in *Situations and Attitudes* (or in *The Liar*), only a small part of it. We record these assumptions below.

Assumption 1.   *A is a set of individuals. R is a set of relations.*

Assumption 2.   *SOA is the set of tuples $\langle\!\langle R_n, a_1, \ldots, a_n \, ; \, i \rangle\!\rangle$ where R_n is a member of R and each a_i $(i = 1$ to $n)$ a member of A. The polarity i is a member of $\{0, 1\}$.*

Definition 1. $SIT = \mathcal{P}(SOA)$, where $\mathcal{P}$ denotes the power set operation.

Definition 2. $PROP = \{p \in \mathcal{P}(SIT) : \forall s, s' \in SIT, \ s \in p$ and $s \subseteq s'$ implies $s' \in p\}$.

Intuitively, $PROP$ is the set of what Barwise and Perry (1983) have called persistent propositions. We will consider only such propositions in our model. The basic idea is that if a situation is a member of a proposition then all its supersets are also members of that proposition.

Definition 3. $\forall s \in SIT, \forall \sigma \in SOA, \ s \models \sigma$ iff $\sigma \in s$.

The relation '$\models$' is called the "holds-in" relation. When $s \models \sigma$ for some situation s and *soa* (i.e. state of affairs) σ we say that σ holds in s.

Definition 4. $\bigvee P \subseteq PROP, \ \bigvee P = \bigcup P$.

Definition 5. $\forall p, p' \in PROP, \ p \wedge p' = \{s \cup s' : s \in p, s' \in p'\}$.

'$\vee$' and '$\wedge$' are the disjunction and conjunction operations for propositions. Disjunction is straightforward, but the conjunction of two propositions is not immediately obvious. Intuitively, we need to operate at the level of the members of propositions to get at the desired operation.

Definition 6. $\forall \sigma \in SOA$, its dual $\bar{\sigma}$ is the same tuple with the opposite polarity.

Propositions have been defined as certain types of sets of situations. A proposition is what gets expressed by an utterance and the intuitive idea behind the above definition for a proposition is that at least one of the situations in the proposition will be factual if the proposition is true. We do not yet have a definition of "factual" or "true" and this is what we define next. We need the concept of a dual and the corresponding closure assumption on SOA for these definitions.

Definition 7. A model $\mathfrak{X}$ of the world is a collection of *soa*s such that for all $\sigma \in SOA$, exactly one of σ and $\overline{\sigma}$ are in $\mathfrak{X}$.

Definition 8. A situation s is factual in model $\mathfrak{X}$ if $s \subseteq \mathfrak{X}$.

Definition 9. A proposition p is true if there is a factual s in p.

A2. Agents

Some situations will have agents in them. We will need just two rational agents $\mathcal{A}$ and $\mathcal{B}$. We assume further that we are given a language $\mathfrak{L}$ that is shared by $\mathcal{A}$ and $\mathcal{B}$. We will take $\mathfrak{L}$ to be a set of sentences.

Assumption 3. $\mathcal{A}, \mathcal{B}$ are two agents.

Assumption 4. $\mathcal{A}, \mathcal{B}$ are rational, that is, they satisfy the axioms of utility theory.

A3. Language

Assumption 5. $\mathfrak{L}$ is a set of sentences.

A4. Actions

We will need two sets of actions, one for $\mathcal{A}$ and one for $\mathcal{B}$. $\mathcal{A}$'s actions will be utterances of sentences. We will use ordered pairs $x = \langle \psi, u \rangle$ to stand for utterances where ψ is a sentence in $\mathfrak{L}$ and u a situation in SIT. $\mathcal{B}$'s actions will be interpretations of $\mathcal{A}$'s utterances. These will be modeled as triples $z = \langle x, p, i \rangle$ where x is an utterance, p a proposition, and i a situation in SIT.

Definition 10. Let $X = \mathfrak{L} \times SIT$ be the set of utterances.

Definition 11. Let $Y = PROP \times SIT$.

Definition 12. Let $Z = X \times PROP \times SIT$ be the set of interpretive acts.

In general, it is crucial to specify both the sentence ψ and the utterance situation u in an utterance $\langle \psi, u \rangle$. The situation u is what provides the context that makes the utterance complete. Each member $\langle x, p, i \rangle$ of Z stands for the act of interpreting the content of x as p in interpretive situation i. When the utterance $\mathcal{B}$ is interpreting is clear from the context (or not needed specifically) we will drop it from the notation and use just $y = \langle p, i \rangle$ to stand for $\mathcal{B}$'s interpretive act.

A5. Relations and States of Affairs

We need some special relations and states of affairs constructed from these relations for the *SDM*. The first is the relation *itc* of intending to convey something. This is a three-place relation with a speaker who does the intending, a proposition that the speaker intends to convey, and an addressee to whom the communication is addressed. The second relation *hu* is the two-place relation of having uttered something. Its first argument is a speaker and its second argument is an utterance. The third relation we need is the relation *hi* of an addressee's having interpreted an utterance as communicating something. This is a three-place relation with arguments an addressee, an utterance, and a proposition.

From these three relations we construct three corresponding sets of states of affairs.

Assumption 6. *itc, a member of R, is the relation "intends to convey."*

Assumption 7. *hu, a member of R, is the relation "has uttered."*

Assumption 8. *hi, a member of R, is the relation "has interpreted."*

Definition 13. $\sigma_{itc} : PROP \to SOA$
$$\sigma_{itc}(p) = \langle\!\langle\, itc, \mathcal{A}, p, \mathcal{B}\, ;\, 1 \,\rangle\!\rangle.$$

These *soas* will be called communicative *soas*.

Definition 14. $\sigma_{hu} : X \to SOA$
$$\sigma_{hu}(x) = \langle\!\langle\, hu, \mathcal{A}, x\, ;\, 1 \,\rangle\!\rangle.$$

Definition 15. $\sigma_{hi} : X \times Y \to SOA$
$$\sigma_{hi}(x, y) = \langle\!\langle\, hi, \mathcal{B}, x, y\, ;\, 1 \,\rangle\!\rangle.$$

A6. Minimal Content

We will also be assuming, as we did in Chapter 2, that the minimal content of an utterance becomes publicly available to $\mathcal{A}$ and $\mathcal{B}$ after the utterance. For this we need a function M mapping utterances into finite sets of propositions. Intuitively, each set $M(\psi, u)$ contains all the possible contents of an utterance of ψ in u. The minimal content of an utterance $\langle \psi, u \rangle$ will then be defined as the finite disjunction of the propositions in $M(\psi, u)$.

Assumption 9. $M : X \to \mathcal{P}(PROP).$

Definition 16. $m : X \to PROP$
$$m(\psi, u) = \bigvee[M(\psi, u)].$$

This completes the building blocks we will need for our construction.

A7. Common Knowledge

We need one final set of assumptions involving common knowledge. As we pointed out in Chapter 2 this is a crucial aspect of communication. We will treat it informally here as we did rationality and relevance above.

Assumption 10. *All the assumptions above are common knowledge between $\mathcal{A}$ and $\mathcal{B}$.*

We turn now to constructing the *SDM*.

3.4 The Strategic Discourse Model

We have already intimated in Chapter 2 how situations can be put together to generate *SDM*s. We constructed the trees representing the various choice structures step by step from initial situations, actions and resulting situations. In carrying out this construction we had to be particularly careful about who had what information at each stage of the game. This led us to an important modification of the traditional structure of incomplete information games. We called the new structure a game of partial information.

We will follow a similar procedure here. We will first construct what we called local games and then construct the global game. It will be most perspicuous to define the set of local games by constructing the elements of the tuple we described in Section 3.1 above one by one. The tuple we construct is $\langle T, \prec\, ; ACT, \alpha\, ; N, \eta\, ; \rho, H, v \rangle$. We will give a brief informal description of each object we construct and what its function is with its definition. The global game is easy to construct once we have the set of local games.

We start with some preliminary remarks. As we emphasized above, the specification of any utterance involves specifying both the sentence uttered and the situation in which it is uttered. Our concern in building the *SDM* is to model certain aspects of this embedding situation as a game. Thus, for our purposes, it is useful to treat it as fixed. Accordingly, in what follows, we will treat it as a parameter. Instead of writing $M(\psi, u)$ and $m(\psi, u)$ we will write $M_u(\psi)$ and $m_u(\psi)$ to mark this assumption. Also, when we deal with *soas* of the type $\langle\!\langle \sigma_{hu}, \mathcal{A}, x\, ; 1 \rangle\!\rangle$ or of the type $\langle\!\langle \sigma_{hi}, \mathcal{B}, x, y\, ; 1 \rangle\!\rangle$ we will replace the x (which is just $\langle \psi, u \rangle$) with the sentence ψ. The situation u will be left out from the notation altogether. (We do this only to keep the notation simple.)

We will also replace the y which is just $\langle p, i \rangle$ with p and drop the i for similar reasons.

B0. Initial Assumptions

Assumption 1. u *is a given factual situation.*

Assumption 2. p^* *is a given true proposition.*

Assumption 3. p^* *is the unique proposition such that* $u \models \sigma_{itc}(p^*)$.

p^* will be the proposition that $\mathcal{A}$ intends to convey to $\mathcal{B}$. We also assume given a finite subset C of $\mathfrak{L}$ called the choice set of $\mathcal{A}$. This is the set of sentences $\mathcal{A}$ actually considers in choosing an optimal utterance. Intuitively, C is intended to be a subset of sentences relevant to the communication.

Assumption 4. C, *a finite subset of* $\mathfrak{L}$, *is* $\mathcal{A}$*'s choice set.*

Assumption 5.   *For all* ψ *in* C, $p^* \in M_u(\psi)$.

This last assumption says essentially that the minimal content of every ψ in $\mathcal{A}$'s choice set is compatible with the intended content p^*. Just as with C, we informally assume that all the members of $M_u(\psi)$ are also relevant (for each ψ in C).

3.4.1   Local Games

B1. Communicative Situations

We start by defining a set of situations called communicative situations. Each communicative situation contains a single communicative state of affairs $\sigma_{itc}(p)$ for some proposition p. These will serve as the initial nodes of the tree of situations we will construct.

Definition 1. $c : PROP \rightarrow SIT$
$$c(p) = \{\sigma_{itc}(p)\}.$$

The situation $c(p)$ is called a communicative situation. Note that by our assumption B0(3) above, $c(p^*)$ is a subset of u.

B2. Consequence Functions

We now make use of the simple observation that every action has a consequence.[1]

---

[1] We use functions and associated operations in the way they are used in logic. Given a function $f : A \rightarrow B$, $\mathrm{dom}(f) = A$ as usual, but $\mathrm{ran}(f) = f[A] = \{f(x) : x \in A\}$. That is, in general, $\mathrm{ran}(f)$ will be a proper subset of (the codomain) B. Also, the inverse of a function is always defined. $f^{-1} = \{(y, x) : (x, y) \in f\}$. Of course, by this definition, f^{-1} will be a function only if f is an injection. Note that $\mathrm{dom}(f^{-1}) = \mathrm{ran}(f)$ and $\mathrm{ran}(f^{-1}) = \mathrm{dom}(f)$. (In other contexts, f^{-1} is defined only when f is a bijection from A to B, and is thus always a function.) We will, in

Definition 2. $f : \operatorname{ran}(c) \times \mathfrak{L} \to SIT$

$\qquad f(s, \psi) = s \cup \{\sigma_{hu}(\psi)\}.$

Definition 3. $g : \operatorname{ran}(f) \times PROP \to SIT$

$\qquad g(t, p) = t \cup \{\sigma_{hi}(\psi, p)\}$ *where* $\psi = 2^{nd}[f^{-1}(t)].$

Both sets of consequence functions map situations into situations. We should point out that the term "consequence" is often reserved for payoffs in some applications of game theory. We are using it to describe the situation that results from an action. It is easy to see how, given initial situations, actions, and their associated consequence functions, we can generate a tree of situations. Note that we have dropped the utterance situation u and the interpretive situation i from the *soas* above (and therefore also from the consequence functions).

B3. Initial Situations

Definition 4. $T_0 : C \to \mathcal{P}(SIT)$

$\qquad T_0(\psi) = \{c(p) : p \in M_u(\psi)\}.$

T_0 is a function that defines, for each ψ in C, a set of communicative situations. Intuitively, these are the initial situations that the addressee $\mathcal{B}$ confronts after he has heard $\mathcal{A}$'s utterance. In the example of Chapter 2, there were two initial situations in the first local game we considered, and just one initial situation in the second local game. Clearly, the number of initial situations in $T_0(\psi)$ must equal the number of propositions in $M_u(\psi)$, since $\mathcal{A}$ could be communicating any of these.

Proposition 1. For all $\psi \in C$, $|T_0(\psi)| = |M_u(\psi)|.$

B4. Speaker's Hypothetical Choice Sets

The next object we construct is the hypothetical choice set of $\mathcal{A}$. Intuitively, this is just the set of sentences that $\mathcal{A}$ might have uttered given that she is in situation $c(p)$. We spell this out in the following way.

Definition 5. $C_\psi : T_0(\psi) \to \mathcal{P}(\mathfrak{L})$

$\qquad C_\psi(s) = \{\gamma \in \mathfrak{L} : c^{-1}(s) \in M_u(\gamma)\}.$

Assumption 6. *For all* $\psi \in C$, *for all* $s \in T_0(\psi)$, *there exists a* $\psi^* \in \mathfrak{L}$ *(that depends on* ψ *and* s*) such that* $M_u(\psi^*) = \{c^{-1}(s)\}.$

We state two trivial consequences of this definition and assumption below.

Proposition 2. $\forall \psi \in C$, $\forall s \in T_0(\psi)$, $\psi \in C_\psi(s).$

Proposition 3. $\forall \psi \in C$, $\forall s \in T_0(\psi)$, $\psi^*(\psi, s) \in C_\psi(s).$

---

what follows, use $\operatorname{ran}(f)$ and f^{-1} in the manner prescribed by logic. (See Enderton 1977.) Note that c is 1-1. This means that c^{-1} is a function.

B5. Resulting Situations

Definition 6. $T_1 : C \to PROP$
$$T_1(\psi) = \{t : \forall s \in T_0(\psi), \ \exists \gamma \in C_\psi(s) \ such \ that$$
$$f(s, \gamma) = t\}.$$

B6. Addressee's Choice Sets

We now construct the addressee's choice sets. These are constrained to be essentially the same as the corresponding minimal content sets. That is, the only propositions $\mathcal{B}$ can infer from $\mathcal{A}$'s utterance are given by the disjuncts that make up the minimal content of the utterance.

Definition 7. $D_\psi : T_1(\psi) \to \mathcal{P}(PROP)$
$$D_\psi(t) = M_u(\gamma) \ where \ \gamma = 2^{nd}[f^{-1}(t)].$$

Proposition 4. $\forall \psi \in C, \ \forall t \in T_1(\psi), \ c^{-1}(s) \in D_\psi(t)$ where $s = 1^{st}[f^{-1}(t)]$.

Proposition 5. $\forall \psi \in C, \ \forall s \in T_0(\psi), \ \exists t \in T_1(\psi), \ D_\psi(t) = \{c^{-1}(s)\}$.

B7. Terminal Situations

Definition 8. $T_2 : C \to PROP$
$$T_2(\psi) = \{t : \forall t' \in T_1(\psi), \ \exists p \in D_\psi(t') \ such \ that$$
$$g(t', p) = t\}.$$

We now construct the tree.

B8. The Tree

Definition 9. $T : C \to PROP$
$$T(\psi) = \bigcup_i T_i(\psi).$$

We have now defined the full set of situations or nodes in each local game. The next step is to define the partial ordering on each $T(\psi)$.

Definition 10. $\forall \psi \in C, \forall t \in T(\psi), \forall t' \in T(\psi), \ t \prec t'$ iff $t \subseteq t'$.

Given the properties of the subset ordering, it follows easily that $\langle T(\psi), \prec \rangle$ is a tree (arborescence) for each ψ in C. We record this below in a proposition.

Proposition 6. $\forall \psi \in C, \ \langle T(\psi), \prec \rangle$ is a tree.

B9. Set of Actions

We are now in a position to define the third element of the game tuple above, the set of actions in the game. This is nothing but the union of all the choice sets defined in B4 and B6.

Definition 11. $ACT : C \to \mathcal{L} \cup PROP$
$$ACT(\psi) = [\bigcup_{s \in T_0(\psi)} C_\psi(s)] \cup [\bigcup_{t \in T_1(\psi)} D_\psi(t)].$$

B10. The "Tree-Action" Map

We can now define the map α that assigns an appropriate set of actions in $ACT(\psi)$ to each noninitial situation in $T(\psi)$.

Definition 12. $\quad \alpha_\psi : T_1(\psi) \cup T_2(\psi) \to ACT(\psi)$
$$\alpha_\psi(t) = 2^{nd}[f^{-1}(t)] \quad \text{if } t \in T_1(\psi)$$
$$= 2^{nd}[g^{-1}(t)] \quad \text{if } t \in T_2(\psi).$$

Definition 13. $\quad \alpha = \{\alpha_\psi : \psi \in C\}.$

α_ψ maps a situation into the action that brings it about.

We now define the player set N and the function η that determines whose turn it is to act.

B11. Players and Turns

Definition 14. $\quad N = \{\mathcal{A}, \mathcal{B}\}.$

Definition 15. $\quad \eta_\psi : T_0(\psi) \cup T_1(\psi) \to N$
$$\eta_\psi(t) = \mathcal{A} \quad \text{if } t \in T_0(\psi)$$
$$= \mathcal{B} \quad \text{if } t \in T_1(\psi).$$

Definition 16. $\quad \eta = \{\eta_\psi : \psi \in C\}.$

η_ψ establishes whose turn it is to act at each decision node.

B12. Initial Probabilities

In general, $\mathcal{A}$ and $\mathcal{B}$ will assign some probability distribution to the set of initial situations $T_0(\psi)$.

Definition 17. $\quad \rho_\psi : T_0(\psi) \to [0,1]$ *such that* $\sum_{s \in T_0(\psi)} \rho_\psi(s) = 1$
$$\rho = \{\rho_\psi : \psi \in \mathfrak{L}\}.$$

B13. Information Sets

We will first define $\mathcal{B}$'s sets and then $\mathcal{A}$'s because $\mathcal{A}$'s information sets are all trivial.

Definition 18. $\quad t \equiv_\mathcal{B} t'$ *if and only if either (1)* $t, t' \in T_0(\psi)$ *or (2) there exist* $s, s' \in T_0(\psi)$ *such that* $t = f(s, \gamma)$ *and* $t' = f(s', \gamma)$ *for some* γ *in both* $C_\psi(s)$ *and* $C_\psi(s')$.

Definition 19. $\quad h^\mathcal{B}_\psi : T(\psi) \to \mathcal{P}(T(\psi))$
$$h^\mathcal{B}_\psi(t) = \{t' \in T(\psi) : t' \equiv_\mathcal{B} t\}$$
$$H^\mathcal{B}_\psi = \{h^\mathcal{B}_\psi(t) : t \in T_1(\psi)\} = T_1(\psi)/\equiv_\mathcal{B}.$$

Definition 20. $\quad h^\mathcal{A}_\psi : T(\psi) \to \mathcal{P}(T(\psi))$
$$h^\mathcal{A}_\psi(t) = \{t\}$$
$$H^\mathcal{A}_\psi = \{h^\mathcal{A}_\psi(t) : t \in T_0(\psi)\}.$$

Definition 21. $H_\psi = H^A_\psi \cup H^B_\psi.$

We should point out that this is not the most general definition of the concept of an information set. For example, we have implicitly assumed that the *SDM* will be a game of perfect information. Our definitions have some simple consequences that we record below.

Proposition 7.   For all $t, t' \in T(\psi)$, $t \equiv_B t'$ implies $\eta_\psi(t) = \eta_\psi(t')$.

This says that all situations in the same information set "belong" to the same player. The same holds for A's information sets trivially.

Proposition 8.   For all $t, t' \in T(\psi)$, $t \equiv_B t'$ and $\eta_\psi(t) = \eta_\psi(t') = B$ implies $D_\psi(t) = D_\psi(t')$.

This says that B has the same choices in those informationally equivalent situations where he has to act.

Proposition 9.   For all $t, t' \in T(\psi)$, $t \equiv_B t'$ implies $t \not\prec t'$.

We now define the payoff functions for A and B.

B14. Payoffs

Definition 22. $v_\psi : T_2(\psi) \to \Re$
$$v^A_\psi = v^B_\psi = v_\psi.$$

We do not impose any special conditions on the payoffs other than assuming they are equal.

B15. Common Knowledge

We have defined all the components of the game tuple. We need one more condition to make this a game, the condition that all the information in each component is common knowledge between A and B.

Assumption 7.   *The information represented by the objects defined above (B1–B14) is common knowledge.*

We now define the set of local games.

B16. Local Games

Definition 23. $LG(\psi) = [T, \prec ; A(\psi), \alpha_\psi ; N, \eta_\psi ; \rho_\psi ; H_\psi ; v_\psi].$

Definition 24. $LG = \{LG(\psi) : \psi \in C\}.$

Ordinarily, we would at this stage have a simple theorem establishing that the object $LG(\psi)$ is a game for each ψ. However, this is not strictly true because the objects we have defined are different from standard games of incomplete information. This is clear from the fact that $LG(\psi)$ depends upon ψ, one of the elements in A's hypothetical choice set. A's optimal choice is determined by the larger structure in which the set LG is embedded, what we have called the global game. B

learns that $LG(\psi)$ is the game $\mathcal{A}$ is playing only after $\mathcal{A}$ has uttered ψ. Thus, $\mathcal{A}$ and $\mathcal{B}$ come to have common knowledge of $LG(\psi)$ only after the utterance. However, $LG(\psi)$ is sufficiently close to a game to justify the term "(local) game." This is why we said at the outset that the game-theoretic tuple would be only the approximate goal of our construction. In fact, $\mathcal{B}$ really has no use for information about the game till it is his turn to play. We call such games local games of partial information. In principle, it is possible to define games of partial information directly as tuples just as games of incomplete information are traditionally defined. This gives us a modified result.

Theorem 3.1. *For all $\psi \in C$, $LG(\psi)$ is a local game of partial information.*

We will now define the global game. Before we do this we need a solution concept for each local game because this is what determines a suitable payoff in the global game. However, from the point of view of exposition it is clearer to assume that some solution concept is available and hence some payoffs and define the global game first. After doing this we will look at the problem of defining a suitable solution concept for the local and global games. This is also what we did in Chapter 2.

3.4.2 The Global Game

The global game is relatively easy to define once we have the collection of local games. The main thing we need to define is the value of each local game, the payoff $\mathcal{A}$ can expect to get if she chooses to play that local game. For now, we will simply assume that such an expected payoff function is available for each game $LG(\psi)$. The intuitive idea is that for each utterance ψ in $\mathcal{A}$'s choice set there is a game $LG(\psi)$ and an associated expected payoff $w(\psi)$ for both $\mathcal{A}$ and $\mathcal{B}$. $\mathcal{A}$'s global decision problem is to choose the ψ that yields the highest payoff.

C1. Initial Situation

Definition 1. *$c(p^*)$ is called the initial situation of the global game.*

Note again that $c(p^*)$ is a subset of u.

Recall that we took $\mathcal{A}$'s choice set C as given in Section 3.3. We need next to define the set of situations resulting from utterances of ψ, for each ψ in C.

C2. The Tree

Definition 2. $GR = \{f[c(p^*), \psi] : \psi \in C\}$.

Definition 3. $GT = \{c(p^*)\} \cup GR$.

Definition 4. *For all t in GR, $c(p^*) \prec t$.*

Trivially, $\langle GT, \prec \rangle$ is a tree.

C3. Payoffs

A provisional assumption:

Assumption* 1. *We assume given a function* $w : C \to \Re$ *mapping local games into payoffs.*

Definition 5. $v : GR \to \Re$
$$v(t) = w(\psi) \text{ where } t = f[c(p^*), \psi].$$

Definition 6. $v^{\mathcal{A}} = v^{\mathcal{B}} = v.$

We define v only to keep definitions of payoffs uniform in the local and global games. In both, payoffs are defined on terminal situations. There is an element of redundancy here, but we will retain it to maintain the uniformity in definitions. The function w will be defined in terms of the solution concept to be defined in the next section.

We are now ready to define the global game.

C4. The Global Game

Definition 7. $GG = [GT, \prec\, ; C\, ; A\, ; v\, ; w]$

Note that no shared knowledge is required of this game.

At first sight this seems more like a situation-theoretic definition of a single-person choice problem. It is almost this except for the last component w. This function brings in the set LG, and with it the full two-person game structure. However, we note in passing that if the payoff v in the definition above were defined directly we would in fact have a situation-theoretic model of a standard single-person choice problem.

C5. The Strategic Discourse Model

Definition 8. $SDM = (GG, LG).$

Theorem 3.2. *The SDM is a game of partial information.*

This gives us the *SDM* of Chapter 2. Note again that there is a redundancy in this definition because LG already appears in GG via its last component w. However, we make LG explicit to emphasize its central role in the larger discourse structure.

3.4.3 Pareto-Nash Equilibrium

Our next step is to define a solution concept for local and global games. As we pointed out in Chapter 2, we do not yet have available a solution concept that provides a unique solution for all local games. We will use the concept of a Pareto-Nash equilibrium as our solution concept.

When there are multiple equilibria, we will allow $\mathcal{A}$ to assume that each equilibrium is equally likely and to use an average value for w. The procedure is first to define solutions for local games, then to define w, and finally to define a solution for the global game. We will call the first type of solution a local solution and the second a (global) solution. The global solution involves essentially a comparison of the available local solutions.

The definition of a local solution involves defining the concept of a strategy, then the concept of a Nash equilibrium, and finally that of a Pareto-Nash equilibrium.

D1. Strategies

A strategy is a function from a player's information sets to some action available in that information set.

Definition 1. $z^{\mathcal{A}}_{\psi,i} : H^{\mathcal{A}}_{\psi} \to C_{\psi}[T_0(\psi)]$
$z^{\mathcal{A}}_{\psi,i}(h^{\mathcal{A}}_{\psi}(t)) = \gamma$ where $\gamma \in C_{\psi}(t)$
$Z^{\mathcal{A}}_{\psi} = \{z^{\mathcal{A}}_{\psi,i} : i = 1, \ldots, n_{\mathcal{A}}\}$.

Definition 2. $z^{\mathcal{B}}_{\psi,j} : H^{\mathcal{B}}_{\psi} \to D_{\psi}[T_1(\psi)]$
$z^{\mathcal{B}}_{\psi,j}(h^{\mathcal{B}}_{\psi}(t)) = p$ where $p \in D_{\psi}(t)$
$Z^{\mathcal{B}}_{\psi} = \{z^{\mathcal{B}}_{\psi,j} : j = 1, \ldots, n_{\mathcal{B}}\}$.

We note here that, strictly speaking, we should prove that our Definitions 1 and 2 above are consistent definitions since they are defined on arbitrary elements of $\mathcal{A}$'s and $\mathcal{B}$'s information sets. We will not bother to spell it out here as it is little more than a trivial consequence of our earlier definitions.

We also do not count the number of strategies available to $\mathcal{A}$ and $\mathcal{B}$, that is, we do not specify the range of the subscripts i and j explicitly. This is easy enough to do but notationally cumbersome and we will leave it as understood. We simply let the number of strategies available to $\mathcal{A}$ be denoted by $n_{\mathcal{A}}$ and to $\mathcal{B}$ by $n_{\mathcal{B}}$.

Definition 3. $z_{\psi,ij} = (z^{\mathcal{A}}_{\psi,i} ; z^{\mathcal{B}}_{\psi,j})$ for $i = 1, \ldots, n_{\mathcal{A}}, j = 1, \ldots, n_{\mathcal{B}}$
$Z_{\psi} = Z^{\mathcal{A}}_{\psi} \times Z^{\mathcal{B}}_{\psi}$.

$z_{\psi,ij}$ is what we called a strategy in the game in Chapter 2. Another term used for strategies in games is strategy profiles. Strategies are defined for each local game $LG(\psi)$ of course. As we had said in Chapter 2, we do not concern ourselves with mixed strategies as pure strategies (that is, strategies of the type we've defined above) suffice for the problems we're looking at.

D2. Expected Payoffs

Based on our definitions of a strategy we define the concept of a Nash equilibrium. As we said in Chapter 2, a strategy is a Nash equilibrium if it doesn't pay to deviate unilaterally. We first redefine the payoffs in terms of strategies and then give the definition. This is just the expected payoff to each player for pursuing a strategy profile $z_\psi = \langle z^{\mathcal{A}}_{\psi,i} \, ; \, z^{\mathcal{B}}_{\psi,j} \rangle$.

Definition 4. $Ev_\psi : Z_\psi \to \Re$
$Ev_\psi(z^{\mathcal{A}}_{\psi,i} \, ; \, z^{\mathcal{B}}_{\psi,j}) = \sum_s \rho_\psi(s) \cdot v_\psi[g[f(s,\gamma),p]]$
$where \; \gamma = z^{\mathcal{A}}_\psi[h^{\mathcal{A}}_\psi(s)] \; and \; p = z^{\mathcal{B}}_\psi[h^{\mathcal{B}}_\psi[f(s,\gamma)]].$

D3. Nash Equilibrium

Definition 5. *A strategy* $z^* = (z^{\mathcal{A}}_{\psi,i}{}^* \, ; \, z^{\mathcal{B}}_{\psi,j}{}^*)$ *is a Nash equilibrium if*
(a) $Ev_\psi(z^*) \geq Ev_\psi(z^{\mathcal{A}}_{\psi,i} \, ; \, z^{\mathcal{B}}_{\psi,j}{}^*)$ *for all* $i = 1, \ldots, n_{\mathcal{A}}$
(b) $Ev_\psi(z^*) \geq Ev_\psi(z^{\mathcal{A}}_{\psi,i}{}^* \, ; \, z^{\mathcal{B}}_{\psi,j})$ *for all* $j = 1, \ldots, n_{\mathcal{B}}.$

Definition 6. *Let* $N^*[LG(\psi)]$ *denote the set of Nash equilibria of the game* $LG(\psi)$.

Note that we have defined the concept of a Nash equilibrium in a somewhat limited way as applying only to the games $LG(\psi)$. It is clearly a much more general concept and can be defined for all games. However, we are not in a position to define the concept more generally because we would first need to define the class of all games situation-theoretically. But it should be easy to see how a more general definition of Nash equilibrium can be given based on Definition 5 above. By Nash's (1951) existence theorem the Nash set N^* is guaranteed to be nonempty. Note however that in general Nash's existence theorem guarantees an equilibrium in the space of mixed strategies, not pure strategies. In the types of coordination games we are considering, we get existence in pure strategy space as well.

Theorem 3.3 (Nash). *For all* $\psi \in C$, $N^*[LG(\psi)]$ *is nonempty.*

D4. Pareto-Nash Equilibrium

In Chapter 2 we discussed some reasons why a Nash equilibrium isn't strong enough as a solution concept for strategic discourse situations. We also pointed out that the many refinements of Nash equilibria that have been explored also fall short of the problem of providing a unique equilibrium for the entire class of games we are considering. We will use the idea of Pareto-dominance to define a Pareto-Nash equilibrium as we did in Chapter 2. This does not solve the problem, but it gives us a refinement of Nash that seems plausible to use in this context.

We need to define the concepts of Pareto-domination and Pareto-Nash equilibrium. In a general setting, one strategy is said to Paretodominate another if no player is made worse off and at least one player is made better off by playing the dominating strategy. For the games we're looking at both players have identical payoffs so that if one player is better off playing a strategy so is the other. This makes the concept of Pareto dominance quite simple in this special case.

A Pareto-Nash equilibrium is, as we said in Chapter 2, a Nash equilibrium that is not Pareto dominated by any other Nash equilibrium.

Definition 7. *For all $\psi \in C$, a strategy z_ψ Pareto dominates another strategy z'_ψ if $Ev_\psi(z_\psi) > Ev_\psi(z'_\psi)$.*

Definition 8. *A strategy is a Pareto-Nash equilibrium if it is a Nash equilibrium and if it is not Pareto dominated by any other Nash equilibrium.*

Definition 9. *Let $PN^*(\psi)$ be the set of Pareto-Nash equilibria.*

Clearly, $PN^*(\psi)$ will be nonempty given that $N^*(\psi)$ is nonempty. However, there is no guarantee that it will be a singleton.

Proposition 10. *For all $\psi \in C$, $PN^*(\psi)$ is nonempty.*

D5. Consistent Pareto-Nash Equilibria

Our next step is to define the expected payoff w for each local game. If we had a solution concept that guaranteed a unique solution concept for each local game, we could define w directly, as the payoff $\mathcal{A}$ could expect from the unique equilibrium strategy. We will have to define w as the average payoff assuming a uniform distribution over $PN^*(\psi)$.

There is also another complication, one that we mentioned in Chapter 2. We need to ensure that the solutions we use are consistent with $\mathcal{A}$'s choice of ψ in the global game. That is, we cannot consider Pareto-Nash equilibria that do not involve ψ in $\mathcal{A}$'s equilibrium strategy. This is because $\mathcal{B}$ constructs $LG(\psi)$ on the assumption that $\mathcal{A}$ has chosen ψ. This means that for at least one s in $T_0(\psi)$, $\mathcal{A}$ must choose ψ as the optimal action. All equilibria that do not involve ψ at all can be regarded as inconsistent. Thus, only consistent Pareto-Nash equilibria must be averaged to define the global payoff function w.

Definition 10. *A Pareto-Nash equilibrium $(z^{\mathcal{A}}_\psi, z^{\mathcal{B}}_\psi)$ is said to be consistent if, for at least one $s \in T_0(\psi)$, $z^{\mathcal{A}}_\psi[h^{\mathcal{A}}_\psi(s)] = \psi$.*

Definition 11. *Let $CPN^*(\psi)$ be the set of consistent Pareto-Nash equilibria.*

Note that it is possible for $CPN^*(\psi)$ to be empty.

D6. Global Payoffs

Definition 12. *Suppose $CPN^*(\psi)$ is nonempty.*

$$TERM: CPN^*(\psi) \to T_2(\psi)$$
$$TERM(z^\mathcal{A}_\psi, z^\mathcal{B}_\psi) = g[f[c(p^*), \gamma], p]$$
$$where \;\; \gamma = z^\mathcal{A}_\psi[h^\mathcal{A}_\psi[c(p^*)]]$$
$$and \; p = z^\mathcal{B}_\psi[h^\mathcal{B}_\psi[f[c(p^*), \gamma]]].$$

TERM picks out the terminal situation t in $T_2(\psi)$ that results from playing out the equilibrium actions starting from the factual initial situation $c(p^*)$. It is the payoff from this terminal situation that is relevant to w.

Definition 13. $w : C \to \Re$

$$w(\psi) = -\infty \;\; if \; CPN^*(\psi) \; is \; empty$$
$$= [1/|CPN^*(\psi)|] \sum_t v(t) \; otherwise,$$
$$where \; t \in \mathrm{ran}(TERM).$$

Once we have the global payoff function, we have to specify how $\mathcal{A}$ solves the global game GG. This is trivial because all $\mathcal{A}$ needs to do is maximize $w(\psi)$.

Definition 14. $C^* = \max{}^{-1}_{\psi \in C} \, w(\psi)$

Proposition 11. C^* is nonempty.

To summarize, $\mathcal{A}$ considers each local game $LG(\psi)$ for each ψ in her choice set C. Solving $LG(\psi)$ gives a payoff function $w(\psi)$ and $\mathcal{A}$ maximizes this to figure out her optimal utterance, say φ. $\mathcal{B}$ is faced with the task of interpreting the optimal utterance φ. $\mathcal{B}$ constructs the local game $LG(\varphi)$ and chooses an optimal interpretation based on the solution set $CPN^*(\varphi)$. If there is more than one consistent Pareto-Nash equilibrium, then $\mathcal{B}$ cannot do better than choose one of these randomly.

We end with two observations. First, is it possible for $CPN^*(\psi)$ to be empty for all ψ in C? This will depend on how C is specified. If, for example, we assume that C contains a ψ^* such that $M_u(\psi^*) = \{p^*\}$ then $CPN^*(\psi^*)$ is a singleton (because $LG(\psi^*)$ is a trivial game). Second, we point out that we do need a solution concept that is more powerful than the one we have considered to avoid the difficult problem of multiple equilibria.

3.5 Conclusion

This concludes our construction. As is evident, we have defined only a small class of the full range of *SDMs* we considered in Chapter 2. We have shown how games of partial information can be constructed from the elements of situation theory and from other objects like rational agents.

We will now turn to some applications of this model. We will, in particular, sketch a new theory of names and descriptions based on the *SDM*.

4

From Meaning to Content

4.1 Introduction

We posed the problem in Chapter 1 of how a speaker can use a shared language to communicate information to an addressee. That is, given the meanings of expressions in a language, how does it happen that a speaker is able in different situations to convey different contents to an addressee with the same expression? How does one get from meaning to content? Our basic answer to this problem is that communication takes place through the mechanism of strategic inference. We looked at one strategic inference in detail in Chapter 2. In Chapter 3 we developed a formal game-theoretic model of this kind of inference. In this chapter we will explore some applications of strategic inference.

It turns out that the model we have developed (and elaborations of it) can be applied to a large variety of cases. It can be applied to the kind of example we looked at in Chapter 2, one where an ambiguous sentence can be disambiguated by a strategic inference if the circumstances of utterance provide the additional information required for the inference. Interestingly, subsentential expressions like descriptions and names can also be viewed in much the same way. For example, a word like "bank" can be used in different ways in different circumstances. This is a relatively simple kind of ambiguity, and it is easy to disambiguate it strategically, within a fairly wide range of circumstances. But we will see in this chapter that it is possible to consider other types of ambiguity strategically as well.

Barwise and Perry (1983) have discussed a number of ways of using definite descriptions. They showed that all these uses could be modeled by treating the interpretation of a definite description as a partial function from situations to individuals. We will show first in Section 4.2 how our conception of strategic inference together with a fundamental relation that we will describe below can give us a systematic account of the class of descriptions. We will see next, in Sections 4.3 and 4.4, that the same picture applies to names as well, and that it provides a simple and elegant approach to a number of puzzles, in particular the famous Fregean puzzle of informative identities. Another important problem concerning names, one that has not received adequate attention, is how a speaker can communicate the intended referent when a name applies to more than one person. We will discuss this problem in some detail (and in a somewhat general setting, to indicate the kinds of issues that are involved) with the *SDM*. This problem, of how the actual communication comes about, is crucial for an understanding of what makes language as flexible as our account shows it to be.

We should emphasize that it has not been possible to attend to many of the important issues connected with these topics that would be necessary in a full discussion.[1] Our purpose here is a much more limited and provisional one. We feel we have a substantially new approach to these issues, one that builds upon the framework of situation theory and game theory, and also on the account given by Barwise and Perry. Our approach is certainly not worked out in sufficient detail to be a full-fledged theory. It might best be called a "picture" in the sense in which Kripke (1977) has used the term, indicating just a potential for a fuller theoretical development. Having said this, however, we should also point out that in certain important respects our account will be seen to be closer to a complete mathematical theory than other accounts that have been put forward, situated as it is in two rich mathematical frameworks.

We start with an account of definite descriptions.

4.2 Definite Descriptions

We present here a theory of the class of linguistic expressions called definite descriptions. Our account builds upon the many fundamental insights of Russell and Strawson, and depends in crucial ways upon the framework of situation theory and strategic interaction developed in Chapter 3.

The theory involves two quite basic ideas. The first idea is that definite descriptions can be used in a number of different ways. And second, there must be some way to communicate the intended use on a particular occasion of utterance.

The idea of the use of a linguistic expression was first brought into theoretical focus by Austin (1975). We do not as yet have a theory of

---

[1] In particular, we do not compare and contrast this account with Partee's (1986) work in the framework of Montague grammar.

this concept that is rich enough to do justice to the subtlety of Austin's investigations. Just as the intuitive notion of meaning conflates many distinct concepts, so does the notion of use. And, to borrow an analogy from Barwise and Perry (1975), just as the number 100 can be broken down into components in several different ways, and just as meaning can be decomposed into distinct concepts, so can the notion of use. We will not attempt to give such an analysis here, but the theory we develop indicates the kinds of distinctions that are needed. In a sense, this entire dissertation can be taken to be about this concept. Situation theory and the theory of strategic interaction (or the theory of games) are indispensable tools for this task.

To develop the first idea, that of different uses of a description, we start with some of the apparatus of situation theory. We will develop the idea informally, using the concepts of situation theory in a "semitechnical" way. There may be more than one way to formalize the idea (and the theory we develop) and we will leave this open here. In Chapter 3, we introduced the ontological concepts of individual, property, and relation that are individuated from situations and states of affairs by agents. We note that we are using the term "ontological" not in any metaphysical or existential sense but simply to refer to a domain of semantical objects. We wish to remain neutral about the underlying metaphysical status of the ontology we put forward. In any case, no implicit defense of a naive realism is intended here.

With this cautionary note, we introduce two more concepts of a similar kind here. The first is the notion of a type of object, the second the notion of the extension of a property (or relation). We will use "property" to include relations as well, in order to avoid having to say the cumbersome "properties and relations" each time.

We refer to properties in two different ways, ascriptively or objectually. That is, we sometimes treat properties as the kinds of entity that are "attached" to other objects, as descriptive of objects. But we also treat properties as objects, especially when we wish to ascribe other properties to an objectually viewed property. Saying that someone is bald involves an ascriptive use of the property of being bald, saying that baldness is unavoidable involves ascribing another property, (that of being unavoidable), to this objectually treated property. We introduce the notion of a type or kind of object as an abstract object obtained by "objectifying" or reifying a property. For example, there are all kinds of situations in the world that have cakes in them. From such situations we can abstract or generate the property of being a cake. We can treat this property objectually and say "The cake is a much-loved object." To mark this way of treating properties we bring in the notion of a type of object. This will allow us to say that, in the sentence above, we are talking about a certain type of object rather than any particular cake. As semantic objects, types are intimately connected with properties. In particular, for every property there is a corresponding type and vice-versa.

The extension of a property in some situation is the collection of objects that has that property in that situation. For example, it is useful (from more than one viewpoint) to contemplate the collection of all objects (in the world, or in some smaller situation) that have the property of being a cake. Given the intimate connection between property and type, we can have extensions of types as well. The extension of a type of object will be the extension of the corresponding property. Situation theory, a small part of which we looked at earlier, is a mathematical theory of the universe of such objects.

We are now ready to present the core of our account of definite descriptions. We will see in particular the crucial role played by the ontological or informational universe we have sketched above.

We develop the idea of use in the following way.

(1) Every definite description is "associated" with a property, or with what Barwise and Perry have called a describing condition.

(2) This associated property is what gets used in different ways in different uses of a description. Properties, being what they are, can be used in a fixed, determinate number of ways. This provides a fundamental ontological constraint on the different ways in which descriptions can be used.

(3) We will first enumerate, very briefly and without examples, six uses of definite descriptions.

One way to use a description and the corresponding property is to refer to some particular object that satisfies this property, to some particular instantiation of the property. Another way is to pick out the particular collection of objects that has the property, the extension of the property. We said above that properties can be treated objectually or ascriptively, and we have two more uses corresponding to this distinction. That is, we can use a property to determine the type of object that has the property. Or we can use it ascriptively to get at the property itself. A fifth way is to fix upon whatever particular individual satisfies the property. A sixth is to pick out whatever particular collection of objects satisfies this property.[2] It should be clear that there must be a fixed number of permutations permitted by our ontology and

---

[2] A seventh use is one in which the property can be used to pick out variably *any* individual member of a collection of objects that satisfies the property. We will not consider this use further in this dissertation.

that this imposes a fundamental constraint on the number of different ways in which a description might be used.

(4) Each type of use of a property results in a different type of proposition being expressed (when the description is part of an appropriate utterance, of course). For each use of a description, a different entity related to the associated property becomes a constituent of the proposition expressed or communicated by the utterance. The entities corresponding to the first four uses in the list above are, respectively, the particular object that instantiates the property, the extension of the property, the type corresponding to the property, the property itself. The fifth use involves both the property and the instantiating object becoming a constituent of the proposition. The last use results in the property and its extension becoming a constituent of the proposition.

(5) The first use we have identified is the one Strawson (1956) focused on and Donnellan (1966) called referential. The second use we will call extensional. The third and fourth uses we will call the reified and predicative uses respectively. The fifth use is the Russellian (1919) attributive use. And we will call the sixth use, a trifle clumsily perhaps, the attributive extensional use. We will give examples of these different uses in a minute.

(6) It seems possible to group these six uses into two classes, the first called the set of designative uses, the other, for lack of a better term, attributive uses. The designative uses all pick out or designate or refer to some entity, be it individual, property, type, or extension. The attributive uses pick out whatever entity (of a particular kind) satisfies the property. Since there are four designative uses, we might expect four corresponding attributive uses. For obvious reasons, however, trying to construct something like an attributive typical use or an attributive predicative use is like applying an identity map. One just does not generate a new use.

To summarize the picture sketched above, what a speaker does when she uses a description in an utterance is to access the property associated with the description and use this property in one of a fixed number of ontologically circumscribed ways. With each different use of this accessed property, she expresses a different proposition (given that some proposition is expressed by the utterance).

A crucial point that we have left implicit so far is that the various entities—properties, individuals, types, and extensions—accessed by the description are determined circumstantially, by the discourse situation and background in which the description is uttered. The entity accessed in a particular use has to be communicated to the addressee in order for the proposition it helps to constitute to be communicated to the addressee. This brings in the second fundamental idea of our theory of descriptions, that of communicating the intended use to the addressee. This idea we develop in the following way.

(7) The particular property accessed by the use of a description, and the particular way in which this associated property is used in an utterance are determined by the constraints imposed by the communicative process. That is, the constraints of situated communication that we modeled with the *SDM* in Chapter 2 and 3 bring in a second set of constraints on the use of a description. We will show below how the *SDM* can be used to model the strategic inference involved in the transfer of the intended use of the description to the addressee.

(8) While all the uses involve the *SDM*, the referential and extensional uses of a description work in a special way. They involve the use of a (typically external) situation that Barwise and Perry (1983) have called the resource situation. This resource situation is what helps speaker and addressee to fix the referent or the extension. Figuring out what the correct resource situation is itself involves a strategic inference. That is, first the addressee has to figure out how the description is being used, what property is being accessed and how that property is being used. If the use is referential or extensional, he has then to figure out what the resource situation is in order to pick out the designated object. All the other uses are relatively "self-contained" in that the associated property suffices to fix its contribution to the proposition.

This difference between the referential and extensional uses and the other four uses is a consequence of the kind of relation that exists between the associated property and the entity it helps to pick out. To find an instance of a property or a collection of objects satisfying the property one needs, in general, to look at the world, or in our universe of partial objects, one needs to look at some situation. Since there are many situations (but just one world) the addressee has to solve the additional problem of figuring out which situation is the correct resource situation. Of course, it is this very partiality that allows a speaker to refer to different instances or different extensions of a property depending on the situation of utterance and the corresponding resource situation.

This, in its bare essentials, is our theory of descriptions. It consists of two fundamental sets of constraints corresponding to the two basic ideas at its core. The first set of constraints are essentially ontological or informational, the second are essentially a product of the strategic interaction between speaker and addressee, and could be called communicative.

To be sure, quite apart from the informal presentation of these ideas, there are many points that need to be clarified and elaborated and we will attend to them after discussing some examples.

Once we become fully situated semanticists, we have to accept a slight awkwardness in presenting any example. In traditional semantics, it sufficed to display a sentence and discuss it. Now we have to, of necessity, say something about the circumstances of utterance, and this will seldom appear quite as neat as a displayed sentence. One way out is to pick examples of a type in which other uses of the description are either impossible or very unlikely (relative to the collection of situations).

Consider the following sentences.

Designative Uses

Referential

(1a) The chair looks comfortable.

(1b) Henry ate the cake.

Extensional

(2a) The chairs look comfortable.

(2b) The lions look hungry.

Reified

(3a) The comfortable chair is difficult to design.

(3b) The comfortable chair does not exist.

(3c) The black hole is a fascinating object.

Predicative

(4a) He is a lawyer.

(4b) This is the doctor.

Attributive Uses

Attributive (Referential)

(5) The plumber will have to fix it.

Attributive (Extensional)

(6) The killers will be apprehended.

The most natural uses for the descriptions in the sentences above include the ones we have indicated, though no doubt there will be circumstances in which they might be used differently. The first pair of sentences could be used to refer to a particular chair and cake in the shared perceptual environment of the speaker and addressee. The second set can clearly be used to refer to a particular circumstantially determined collection of chairs and lions. Notice that we have had to pluralize the nouns. This suggests something important about the class of expressions we are calling descriptions, and we will comment on it below.

In the third set of sentences illustrating the reified use, it seems clear that the speaker is not referring either to a particular chair or black hole but is designating the relevant property objectually. Sentence (3b) shows how we can interpret negative existential sentences in a natural way without running into any of the traditional problems and paradoxes that arise if we allow only referential uses of noun phrases.

The fourth set can be used to describe the individual picked out pronominally or demonstratively. Consider an appropriately used sentence of the form "Smith is the doctor." Here, it is unlikely (because inefficient, a point we will return to below) that the description is being used referentially to say that Smith is Smith. In some circumstances it could be used attributively, as when, for example, A and B have already been talking about the doctor. It is clear, however, that there are situations in which A would be stating that Smith has the property of being the doctor. This is no different from an appropriate utterance of "Smith is happy."

The fifth and sixth attributive uses are about whatever individual and collection satisfies the relevant property, either of being a plumber or a killer. It is not obvious how these attributive uses differ from the corresponding referential uses. Consider the extensional case. There are two ways of specifying a set, by listing its members or by the method of "abstraction," that is, by specifying the property or condition its members must satisfy. Our extensional use is similar to the first method of enumeration, and the attributive extensional use to the method of abstraction. The referential use is in an important respect different from the enumerative method, however. We need to distinguish between two sorts of enumeration, the kind involved in set theory which is a part of language and the kind of "enumeration" involved in an extensional use which is a part of the world. When A uses "$\{1, 2, 3\}$" in an utterance she enumerates the collection linguistically. When A uses "the lions" extensionally, she designates ("enumerates") a collection of lions via a resource situation in the world. This is a rough sort of "enumeration" because it may not be possible to explicitly list all the members as the set-theoretic method of enumeration requires. (The counterpart of set-theoretic enumeration would be a list of appropriate noun phrases in an utterance. There cannot be a "referential" enumeration for a collection of numbers!) This shows incidentally the kinds of choices that language and reality provide for making statements. To talk about a collection of objects in the world, one can either explicitly build it up one by one linguistically, or use a single term extensionally, or again use a term in the attributive extensional way.

The discussion above provides a new way of viewing the traditional referential and attributive distinction for individuals. The referential use is like the enumerative method and the attributive use like the method of abstraction, except that we are dealing here with different ways of specifying an individual rather than a class or set. Interestingly, this difference, that we are dealing with the specification of an individual rather than a class, has the consequence that there are now no longer two sorts of enumeration. Getting to the individual via a "list" of terms and getting to it via a single "extensionally" (i.e. referentially) used term amount to roughly the same thing. Not only does the distinction between the two methods of specifying a set illuminate the referential and attributive distinction for individuals but the illumination goes the other way as well. The properties of each distinction clarify the other. For example, there is a question about whether the sets specified in the two ways are the same or not. Extensional set theory identifies the two, but this is not the only way to go. But if we choose the "intensional" route we would probably have to go the same way with individuals as well, a matter about which we seem to have clearer extensional intuitions. The referential-attributive distinction has also been explored from the point of view of utterances rather than sentences. This should make it easier to see mathematics as an activity.

This also suggests a better way to see why it doesn't make sense to talk of referential and attributive uses for types and properties. As far as properties go, once we have a property, we have it. There are no two "methods" of specifying a property. The case of types is more interesting. We specify a type via a property, just as we do individuals and extensions. So it seems that we may have a similar distinction here. But it appears difficult to find clear examples. One criterion often invoked to illustrate the referential-attributive distinction is that in a referential use the description itself is inessential whereas in an attributive use it is essential. (There are many problems with this criterion, not least its imprecision, and as stated it is in fact false. We will touch upon this briefly below.) If we say "The black hole is fascinating" could we be using the description in a dispensable way? It appears not, and this has to do with the rather intimate relation that exists between properties and types, a relation that we have considered only informally, however. Though types of objects (like individuals) have many properties (for example, of being fascinating) they have one property that is very special, the property that they are "objectifications" or typifications of. This makes them quite different from both individuals and extensions. This is perhaps one way of arguing that there cannot be two different ways of getting at a type.

To return to our examples, in each of them some property (circumstantially) associated with the description is used to get at a related entity in a particular way, which becomes a constituent of the proposition expressed.

It is important to emphasize that these are fundamentally different uses. As we said above, these differences can be identified partially by the different ways in which the describing condition contributes to the proposition that gets communicated in each case. Of course, the same description could, in other circumstances, be used in a quite different way. Our concern is simply to point out that there are situations in which the description is used in the particular way we are identifying.

Some of our examples did not involve definite descriptions, seen as a subclass of the class of singular terms. In particular, the two extensional uses were not exemplified by a definite description. It is not clear if such uses can be found with singular definite descriptions. This suggests two things. The first is that though the class of singular definite descriptions may be important to isolate, it may not be possible to give a theoretical account of this subclass in isolation. Perhaps the natural class to look at is the entire class of descriptions. Notice that in our account no special role was identified for the determiner "the." This suggests that the account should go through for other types of descriptions as well. The sentence (4a) hints at this. The second point our observation above suggests is the need for an account of "the." It should be the determiner that prevents (or makes rare) a particular sort of use. Other determiners, or quantifiers generally, should impose other sorts of restrictions to eliminate some of the possible uses generated by the noun alone.

To summarize the above, we might say that we have given a partial account of the class of all descriptions. A more complete account would need a theory of how the various quantifiers work, using this term broadly to include the standard sorts of terms that qualify the noun or description in a quantitative way. We include in this class terms like "the" and "a," "every," "no," "some," "most," and the like, and also terms like "two" (as in "two astronauts").

This suggests that a complete account would require a careful study of the full set of possible uses of descriptions together with a study of the kinds of restrictions brought in by quantifying terms to eliminate some of these uses. The uses that remain have to be further reduced to one to get at a single proposition. We will look at how this further reduction takes place in a later section.

We should point out that the key idea of our account is that the possible uses of a description are fixed in a precise sort of way by the logical structure of the world. We have identified six (or seven) uses. A closer scrutiny may reveal more, or even perhaps less. Our point is that there is a principled way to make such decisions, not based on examples alone. Without such a method one could in principle imagine the possibility of an indefinite number of uses to be found by examining more examples. Of course, finding examples is crucial even for our kind of account because the principal source of evidence about this domain of logical entities is linguistic.

Let us call each of the six kinds of operation that one can perform on a property corresponding to the six uses an ontological transformation. We might name them, respectively, the operations of instantiating, ("enumerative") extensionalizing, reifying, identity, attributive instantiation, and (abstractive or attributive) extensionalizing. When applied to a property, this set of six transformations generates a set of entities that we will call the set of transforms of the property.[3]

---

[3]This idea admits of interesting connections with situation theory and we include a few tentative remarks in this direction. It is unclear at this stage whether this is the best way to formalize these ideas.

Let's call the collection of all the entities of situation theory an ontological space. Entities like properties, individuals, types, and extensions certainly belong to this space, and so do more basic entities like situations and states of affairs. We can then define a set of (possibly partial) transformations on this ontological space. And we can study both the underlying ontological space and the space of transformations, just as we may study an Euclidean space and its group of, say, rotations about an axis. At present, situation theory can be conceived of as a theory of the underlying space of ontological entities. Once this space is fully developed, we can abstract from it and study spaces of transformations on it.

It is interesting that, unlike the case of Euclidean and many other spaces, we do not have the ontological space available to us in any obvious way. Our primary routes to discovering the objects that populate this space are linguistic and epistemic situations, and also some intuitive ideas about how we might transform an entity to generate another entity. That is, in an important sense, we have to discover both the underlying ontological space and its associated space of transformations more or less simultaneously. This is reflected partly by the need to define one collection of entities in terms of another, for example, properties in terms of states of affairs, or

Each entity when ontologically transformed will generate a subset of the set of ontological entities. Let this subset be denoted by $O(P)$ when the transformed entity is the property P. That is, $O(P)$ contains the six transformations applied to the property P. We will call $O(P)$ the ontological transform of P. Note that, in general, these transformations are situated transformations, and to make this fully explicit, we could write $O(P, s)$ where s is the situation relative to which the transform is to be evaluated. In the case of the operations of instantiating and extensionalizing this situation is the external situation called a resource situation.

Let's now look at the six uses in some more detail.

In the referential and the extensional uses, the associated property or describing condition serves to identify the referent via a resource situation. That is, there is some shared situation between $\mathcal{A}$ and $\mathcal{B}$, typically one that is perceptually accessible or one that has been built up by previous discourse. This resource situation contains an object satisfying the describing condition. And this property of the shared resource situation makes it possible for $\mathcal{A}$ to communicate her intended reference to $\mathcal{B}$.

In the corresponding attributive uses, the property associated with the description plays a direct role in identifying an individual or extension. As Barwise and Perry (1983) have pointed out, the describing condition is itself a constituent of the content of the utterance. The referent or extension is simply whatever object has the attribute in question.[4] In general, the addressee is unlikely to know what object the property picks out, and indeed, this is unnecessary for the communication to take place. For example, neither the speaker nor the addressee need to know who the plumber is in order to describe a situation which supports the fact that the plumber, whoever he is, will have to fix it. Or, $\mathcal{A}$ might communicate to $\mathcal{B}$ that $2^{2^4}+1$ is a (Fermat) prime without either of them knowing what the number is. What is happening is that there are two different propositions being expressed in a referential and attributive use of the same description even though their truth conditions may be the same (ignoring the kinds of errors that may occur in a referential use that Kripke (1977) and Donnellan (1966) have pointed out). In an attributive use, if an addressee can identify the referent that

---

types in terms of properties. But we can also consider these two spaces abstractly, as independent but related mathematical structures.

[4]This object will also satisfy the attribute relative to a situation, as in the referential cases. We do not deal with this here except to point out that it requires us to consider a different type of proposition that Barwise and Etchemendy (1986) have called an Austinian proposition.

is an additional bonus. The associated property picks out an individual or extension but in a way that makes it plausible to say, in a rough sort of way, that the utterance is more about the property than about the individual or collection picked out.

The predicative use differs from the uses above in designating the property itself, rather than some object directly or indirectly identified by the property. The describing condition is once again a constituent of the content, as it is in an attributive use, but here it is so "directly." In the attributive use it enters into the content indirectly, to provide a condition for the denoted individual to satisfy (see Barwise and Perry 1983). (Incidentally, the use Barwise and Perry have called appositive ("Smith, the doctor, looks happy") appears to be a special case of the predicative use.)

The reified use picks out the generic object or type of object having the relevant property, and this is what makes it into the content.

We can draw the following rough pictures to summarize the ways in which descriptions work.

resource situation

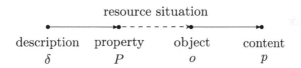

description	property	object	content
δ	P	o	p

FIGURE 4.1 Referential and Extensional Use

A referential use of δ (Figure 4.1) is (circumstantially) associated with the property P. A circumstantially (strategically) inferred resource situation has an object o satisfying this property in general. But it is possible for o to fail to satisfy P and yet for the addressee to figure out that o is the intended referent. Schematically expressed, the arrow connecting P to o is a "nonrigid" connection. Once the correct o has been inferred it alone makes it into the content.

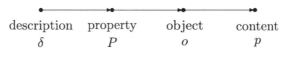

description	property	object	content
δ	P	o	p

FIGURE 4.2 Attributive Uses

An attributive use of δ (Figure 4.2) is also (circumstantially) associated with P. Here, however, the denoted object must satisfy P. This requirement has the consequence that P enters p indirectly, as a condition on o. Schematically, the connection between P and o is "rigid."

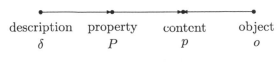

description	property	content	object
δ	P	p	o

FIGURE 4.3 Predicative Use

In a predicative use of δ (Figure 4.3) there is no intervening object and P enters p as a direct constituent. Of course, this use does involve predicating P of some object o, but o comes not from the resource situation (and from the use of δ) but from another part of the utterance (situation). This picture suggests, incidentally, that such pictures can be composed to yield a graph of how each component act of an utterance contributes to the content of the utterance. We will return to this generalized technique later.

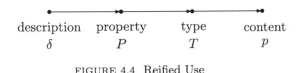

description	property	type	content
δ	P	T	p

FIGURE 4.4 Reified Use

The last picture (Figure 4.4) ought to be more or less self-explanatory by now.

These pictures bring out clearly some of the similarities and differences between the six uses. The property (describing condition) can be seen to play a central but different role in each of these uses. The pictures illustrate, in particular, one of the distinguishing features of referential and extensional uses, the circumstantial relation between the describing condition and the referent. Since only o enters p in this use, there is a relatively weak link between P and p so that an altogether different P and therefore δ would do as well, as long as the same object gets picked out. This circumstantial link between property and described object is best understood by looking at the corresponding transformations involved. These two transformations that we have called instantiation and extensionalization are the ones that involve a resource situation, the ones that are not "self-contained." It is this "externality" that makes the relation between property and described object a circumstantial one. And it is this circumstantiality that results in the weak or "nonrigid" link between the two, allowing for certain types of error. In all the other cases, we have a rigid link between property and transform because no "externality" is involved.

Referential uses are often distinguished from attributive uses on the basis of the description being said to occur "inessentially" in the first, and "essentially" in the second. The picture above shows that this sort of identification is not quite correct. It is the "inessentiality" (or circumstantiality) of the associated property rather than of the description that is the distinctive feature of referential uses. The description is in fact inessential (that is, has a circumstantial relation to the associated property) to all six uses. This is because the situated and strategic nature of utterances often allows an addressee to figure out what a speaker is attempting to communicate even when the linguistic expression appears inadequate or incorrect for the job. Given the right circumstances, even an inarticulate and meaningless mumble will do the job. Essentially, what is needed is that $\mathfrak{SDM}(\varphi, d, B)$ remain constant, however φ or anything else under the speaker and (addressee's control) is varied. On the other hand, it is only when the particular transformation is a circumstantial one that there is room for additional error or flexibility: if, for example, the resource situation is clear, and there is some individual in it that is salient for both speaker and addressee, then almost any associated property could be used to get at it.

We can combine the pictures above into one composite picture (Figure 4.5). This will illustrate clearly what the communicative task is for the speaker and addressee.

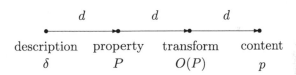

$$\begin{array}{cccc} d & d & d & \\ \text{description} & \text{property} & \text{transform} & \text{content} \\ \delta & P & O(P) & p \end{array}$$

FIGURE 4.5 Linguistic Representation

This diagram shows that there are broadly three problems that need to be solved. First, the associated property has to be obtained. Next, the transform of this property has to be evaluated. Finally, a particular member of $O(P)$ has to be selected for the content. All three problems are to be solved relative to the discourse situation d.

This is where our model of situated communication and strategic inference comes in. The family of acts that are variously called reference, denotation, designation, and the like are just component joint acts of the larger joint act of communication they bring about (together with other component acts). As such, they are built up from the same constituent acts situated and structured in the same way.

That the same description can be used in the different ways described above is just a special case of the general efficiency of (situated) language, and so can be readily accommodated within the *SDM*. It turns out that it is not possible to solve these problems in isolation from the larger utterance in which the description is embedded. This should be obvious because the same description can be used in different ways and it is only the rest of the utterance that can provide the information to figure out which use is the intended one.

This completes our informal account of how descriptions work. The theory consists of two key ideas, that of ontologically constrained uses and that of the situated communication of the intended use on a given occasion. We should emphasize that the second idea is best seen as just an instance of the general efficiency of language. It is a remarkable fact, if it is a fact, that the circumstances of utterance and the rules of language allow for such flexibility in the use of language. We will look at this important phenomenon in some detail in the sections below.

There are some important issues connected with definite descriptions and we discuss a couple of them below to indicate how our general account might be used to address various problems.

Kripke (1977), Linsky (1967), and Donnellan (1966) have pointed out there is a problem in determining what has been said by a speaker in cases where the description is used referentially and the describing condition does not fit the referent.

The theory of definite descriptions we have sketched allows us to clarify the difficulty involved in determining what proposition the speaker has expressed when she uses a description referentially and the describing condition doesn't fit the referent. There are three cases to consider here and all three are instances of a more general problem that has to do communication as such. The transfer of information from A to B may or may not be successful, and if successful, the speaker may have used a misdescription intentionally or accidentally. If A's misdescription is intentional and the transfer is successful, we have a clear case of communication, it is clear what the content of the utterance is, and we can equally clearly assign a truth-value to it. Whether we choose to report what A said with the same misdescription or not will obviously depend on the discourse situation *we* are in, though there are other important issues that need to be considered here.

If the misdescription is unintentional ("the man drinking champagne") and the transfer successful we are faced with a terminological question that applies to all actions. We all know of instances when we goofed in an attempt to do something but still succeeded in doing it owing to some circumstantial reasons that we did not (fully, at least) anticipate. Should we call such an act successful? We are certainly tempted to, keeping our true plans, intentions, and attempt a secret. But such a choice leads to many problems, not the least of which is dishonesty. It would also be unfair to deny ourselves the good luck, rare as it might be. We may as well recognize both facets of this serendipity and call it, a trifle unimaginatively perhaps, a case of accidental success (or communication or reference, in our problem). And with this qualification in mind we could once again specify the proposition communicated and its truth-value.

When the transfer is unsuccessful, the problem becomes a little messy. We have to locate the cause of the failure in order to allocate the blame. Either A or B or both or neither may be culpable, or there may be more than one way to allocate blame. When it is possible to say that exactly one of them has respected the constraints on communication then we should be inclined to say that the proposition identified by this person is the proposition expressed by the utterance, and it is this content whose truth we have to assess. There is a possible divergence here between what the speaker wanted to say and what she did in fact say. In all the other cases no proposition can be clearly identified as the content of the utterance. Obviously, the question of its truth-value does not arise.

Attributive uses of descriptions, and indeed all instances of communication and miscommunication can be handled likewise. Of course, there is an element of arbitrary stipulation in all this, and it is possible for different social groups to choose different conventions or, as seems partly to be the case, to leave it to the discretion of speaker and addressee in ordinary circumstances where the relevant costs are marginal. (In situations where costs do matter, like many litigious situations, the legal system would have to make a relatively explicit stipulation. Of course, such a stipulation cannot be fully explicit without being overly arbitrary because no legal system has as yet an adequate conception of communication!)

To turn to another problem, Martinich (1984) has made the point that the distinction between referential and attributive uses is an epistemological one. Attributive uses are just referential uses in a situation where the speaker or the addressee or both have no other way to identify the denoted individual.

This epistemological objection seems false. It is possible to use a description attributively even when the speaker and addressee have other means to identify the denoted individual. For example, A may want to establish that Jones is insane, and may utter (attributively) "The murderer of Smith (whoever he is) must be insane" to establish the fact that anyone who murdered Smith is insane. She may then use the publicly known fact that Jones is the murderer of Smith to go on to establish Jones's insanity. There is clearly no epistemological indigence here that forces A to an attributive use.

We end this section by observing that we have not given any clear indication of exactly what class of linguistic expressions our theory accounts for. We said above that it is certainly wider than the class of definite descriptions. This is in part confirmed by the fact that there are languages that do not have a definite article. That is, the work done by "the" in English is done differently in other languages. This raises some interesting questions, the most important of which is perhaps how one might go about defining the class of descriptions.

We turn now to names.

4.3 Names

Names appear to be quite simple at first sight but they pose a number of rather subtle problems, most of which were first brought to light by Frege (1892/1980). Perhaps the most famous of these is the puzzle of informative identity statements, how identity statements like "Cicero is Tully" can differ in cognitive value from trivial statements like "Cicero is Cicero." It is partly to meet the challenges posed by this and related problems (existence statements and attitude reports) that Frege was driven to develop his influential semantical theory of sense and reference.

The theory of names we develop also builds upon that of Barwise and Perry (1983) and comes from taking the perspective of situated strategic communication as fundamental. We have already seen the role of efficiency in our treatment of definite descriptions. We will see how a similar view enables us to give a rather natural solution to two of these puzzles as well as a relatively complete theory of names. Our account of names follows rather simply from our account of descriptions and, as such, draws upon the framework of situation theory and strategic inference. In a certain sense, the theory of names we develop can be seen as vindicating a relatively casual remark of Russell's about how ordinary names work.

There are two major approaches to proper names, the "description" theory of names developed by Frege (1892/1980), Russell (1919), and Searle (1958), and the "direct reference" theory developed by Kripke (1980), Donnellan (1966), Evans (1973), and others. Both accounts provide many important insights but implicitly assume that names can be used only referentially (barring a few insightful comments by Russell). This implicit assumption is perhaps a direct consequence of the general tendency of attempting to interpret sentences rather than situated utterances. Kripke's arguments against the description theory are certainly persuasive. However, attending to the fact that names, like descriptions, can be used in multiple ways, and isolating a special property of names to play the role of the property that gets transformed allows us to give an alternative account that succeeds in combining the strengths of the two standard theories without inheriting their weaknesses. We point out again that this is a vast topic and we do not present anything like a mathematically complete account. The central new feature of our account is that names can also be used in more than one way and that it is the flexibility afforded by this fact that gives us a new picture of how names work.

A key element in our theory, pointed out by Barwise and Perry (1983), is the special property associated with every name "N," that of being named "N" (or put less directly, but more in line with our account of descriptions, of being an N). That every name is (circumstantially) associated with such a property is obvious. However, historically, it appears that few theorists have given this important property its due. Barwise and Perry are among the few who have emphasized this neglect. Others who have considered this property favorably are Kneale (1962) and Burge (1973).

Our basic claim is that names are not in principle different from descriptions, and an adequate theory of names must recognize that names can also be used in a number of ways. There does not seem to be any evidence that suggests that names, unlike descriptions, are inefficient. The different uses of names depend perhaps in more subtle (though also perhaps more obvious, once they are pointed out) ways upon the discourse situation. Essentially, it is the special property of being named "N" that gets used in different ways.

Suppose A says to B, "Voltaire is (Francois-Marie) Arouet," in a situation in which they have been discussing Voltaire. Here, "Voltaire" is used referentially. But "Arouet" is used predicatively, and designates its associated property "is named 'Arouet.'" The content of this utterance is not the trivial identity proposition but the proposition that Voltaire is (also) named "Arouet." If A says "If Arouet were Voltaire, he would be the author of Candide," she uses both names referentially, and the description predicatively (at least in some common circumstances). And if B responds with "But Arouet is Voltaire," he uses both names attributively, the attributes being being named such and such. In other words, he has said that the individual named Arouet is identical with the individual named Voltaire.

An utterance of "January has 31 days" involves what we have called a reified use. We could also say "Not all Februaries have 28 days" and this might involve an extensional use of the name. On the other hand, a sentence like "Most Aristotles are Greek" probably (that is, relative to the collection of situations) involves an attributive extensional use of "Aristotle" (and a predicative use of "Greek.")

In our account, just as with definite descriptions, every name has associated with it a property. The description theorists were right in focusing on properties. However, the relevant property to consider is the special property that always goes with having a name. And it is this property that gets exploited in different ways in the six uses, not some intermediate identifying description. This property too needs a name, and we may as well call it the nominal condition in analogy with our account of descriptions.

In a referential use, the nominal condition is used to pick out a particular individual. Here too, as Kripke has pointed out, the name may not fit the referent, or in our terms, the referent may fail to satisfy the nominal condition. A may say to B, "Jones is raking the leaves," and may succeed in communicating her reference to Smith in the appropriate circumstances. Whether or not the nominal condition is satisfied, it does not appear in the content of the utterance, either directly or indirectly. Only the referent does. In other words, referential (and extensional) uses of names are no different from referential (and extensional) uses of descriptions with respect to the contents of utterances containing them. Used attributively, a name picks out whoever or whatever satisfies the nominal condition. This makes the condition a constituent of the content in attributive uses of names, as with descriptions. Predicative uses of names designate the associated property itself and thus involve the nominal condition directly. And reified uses involve the corresponding types.

Given an utterance containing a name the addressee's task is, as before, to figure out which use was intended, and if this use is referential or extensional then to access the correct resource situation. Figuring out the intended use involves the same strategic procedure as in the case of descriptions.

It is important to point out that we do need a resource situation for the referential and extensional uses. There is simply no way to go "directly" from the name to the referent, as Barwise and Perry have pointed out. We have to go via the associated condition, exactly as we do with definite descriptions.

In cases where only one person answers to the name, like Voltaire, the resource situation is just the whole world. With many names, however, this will not do. There are many Bills in the world and so in general we will need to access a smaller resource situation to figure out which Bill the utterance is about. This is exactly like the case with descriptions. "The author of Candide" goes through with the entire world as the resource situation, but "the chair" requires the addressee to infer which resource situation is intended. We will look at the important question of nonunique names (and descriptions) in some detail below.

This completes our brief sketch of the main ideas involved in our theory of names. Before we consider how it solves two important puzzles, let us summarize its key points.

Neither names nor descriptions can be understood without a strategic perspective. Both are efficient and can be used in a number of different ways. As we have seen, these are limited in a fundamental way by the logical structure of the world. Each type of expression is associated with a special property, called the nominal condition in one case and the describing condition in the other. This special property or condition is used in the same way for both names and descriptions but differently in each of the six uses. The referential and extensional uses in particular require one to access and exploit the appropriate resource situation. For a particular use to be communicated a number of conditions need to be satisfied, conditions embedded in the strategic interaction between speaker and addressee.

Though many questions remain our theory does seem, in certain respects at least, to be more complete than either the description theory or the direct reference theory. We show (in Section 4.5 below) how this theory handles the question of nonunique names. A second strength lies in its giving a unified account of a large class of noun phrases.

Its third strength lies in the natural and commonsense solutions it provides for a number of old and recalcitrant conundrums. We will consider two. The first has to do with existence statements, the second with informative identity statements. We will show how our theory solves both problems. The first puzzle will be dealt with briefly. We will consider the second one in some detail. We will show that not only does this problem yield to a particularly simple solution, but that it also accounts for aspects of identity statements that appear to pose difficult if not insuperable problems for both the description theory and the direct reference theory.

When uttered, existential sentences like "N does not exist" typically have a content in which the name is being used in either an attributive or typical way. The key thing is that the name cannot be used

in a referential way in such an utterance. It is only with such uses that
the various puzzles about nonexistent objects and the like arise. If the
name is used attributively for example, then the content would be that
the individual named "N" does not exist. It amounts to saying that a
certain property does not have an instantiation (in a certain situation).
Reified uses are to be handled similarly, as we suggested above with the
reified use of the sentence "The comfortable chair does not exist." Here
we are saying that a particular type of object is not instantiated. In
fact, all singular terms (and even general terms, as in "unicorns don't
exist") pose similar problems and can be handled in the same way.

  With this somewhat brief solution, we turn to the second puzzle.

4.4 Identity and Information

Frege's puzzle, how an utterance of "Voltaire is Arouet" can be informative, yields to a natural solution once we take the situated strategic
perspective seriously. The reader may by now have already guessed the
main ideas of our approach.

  We must first figure out which use is intended by the speaker. In
the standard case (or at least in the situation we described above),
the proposition expressed and communicated is that Voltaire is (also)
named "Arouet." This is a very different proposition from the trivial
(that is, uninformative) identity proposition that Voltaire is Voltaire.
Frege's puzzle arises because these two propositions are wrongly identified. The first proposition (that Voltaire is named "Arouet") is certainly informative. The second proposition is clearly not so. On the
other hand, the first proposition does not express an identity whereas
the second one does. Confusing the two different contents makes it possible to select one property of each, informativeness and expressing an
identity, and then to ask how we could have an informative identity.

  Informative identities are not puzzling by themselves, of course. It
is easy to imagine a situation in which "Arouet" is used attributively
rather than predicatively in the utterance above. In this case, we do
have an identity statement (Voltaire is identical with the individual
named "Arouet") that is also informative. But this is no different from
the discovery that the inventor of bifocals was the first Postmaster
General of the US. Here too, the second description is intended to be
used attributively (and, in most situations, the first description as well).

  The problem with informative identities arises when both the
names in the sentence are used referentially. The very same problem
arises if we try to imagine a situation in which both descriptions in the
(bifocal) sentence above are used referentially. That is, the problem

has to do with a certain combination of uses of singular terms rather than being a peculiarity of names. And, as should be obvious, such a combination of uses cannot yield an informative identity as the content of the utterance. Precisely because the content is trivial, it will be (almost) impossible to find an ordinary situation in which maximizing agents say "Voltaire is Arouet" intending to express the trivial, that is, uninformative identity proposition.

To consider an apparently more dramatic kind of case, it isn't difficult to imagine situations in which "Voltaire is Voltaire" is used informatively. For example, we could have a large discourse situation in which A and B are arguing about whether Voltaire was really named "Voltaire." And A might assert "Voltaire is Voltaire." Not only that, B could retort with "Voltaire isn't Voltaire" and also be expressing a quite coherent and informative proposition. (We can vary the context a bit and imagine a Thorndyke or a Poirot pronouncing, at the end of an investigation, "The butler did it, but the butler isn't the butler." And so on.) Such examples appear to pose problems for both the description theory and the direct reference theory. For the utterances above to be informative the second occurrence of the name (or description) has to be predicative or attributive (and the first referential), and neither theory recognizes either of these uses. It is an added strength of our theory that it handles such examples as naturally as it does the traditional ones.

Of course, in order to really have a complete argument we must be able to show that two referential uses cannot occur in an (informative) utterance of "Voltaire is Arouet." Given the range of situations available to us such a knockdown argument is not possible. But we can come pretty close to it by pointing out that in "almost all" discourse situations a speaker can convey the same "null" content simply by remaining silent, a cheaper choice of action. Unless the speaker wishes to implicate something, in which case the intended content is no longer trivial, it is optimal for the speaker to remain silent. But we have to remain content with the quantifier "almost all" because experience suggests that it is almost always possible to concoct situations that can make the utterance of almost anything optimal. In any case, the puzzle loses much of its force because we have an alternative explanation that resolves it while simultaneously providing an account of names that is both intuitively plausible and that fits in with our larger theory.

It is when we (counterfactually) assume the possibility of referential uses of the two names in "Voltaire is Arouet" and, more importantly, conflate the trivial and informative contents mentioned above that we are led inescapably, as Kripke showed, to the startling conclusion that there are synthetic necessary truths known a posteriori.

If the uses of the descriptions in the bifocal sentence above are taken as referential we are once again led ineluctably to the same surprise. Kripke's discovery that it is important to distinguish the ontological notion of necessity from the epistemological notion of aprioricity and also from the linguistic notion of analyticity is crucial. But "Voltaire is Arouet" does nothing to upset our complacent conflation of these concepts, considered in any of its uses. If "Arouet" is used predicatively, neither a necessary nor an analytic truth is expressed, and the proposition has to be known a posteriori. This is no different from an utterance of "Voltaire is French." If "Arouet" is used attributively, we once again have a contingent, synthetic and a posteriori truth. And if both names are used referentially we have a trivial truth that is analytic, necessary, and knowable a priori.[5]

So far, our account has, I hope, supported relatively conventional intuitions. It is time to point out briefly a rather surprising consequence of the theory. Mathematical identities have been usually taken to be the archetypal referential sentences. If we do take "$2 + 2 = 4$" referentially, we have the now familiar problem of trivial contents. If we view mathematics as an activity, and in particular, the linguistic expression of mathematical propositions and proofs as a type of communicative activity (the speaker and addressee do not need to be distinct) then we should be looking at utterances not sentences, as with all communication. And we can then interpret "$2 + 2 = 4$" as containing not a referential but an attributive use of the first noun phrase "$2 + 2$." (The sum of two and two is equal to four.) This would explain how mathematical identities can be informative. Of course, they still remain necessary truths, (unlike "Hesperus is Phosphorus" when used attributively) and the question of how necessary truths can be informative is a different one. But the first step to answering it is to make clear that the content of mathematical utterances is at least not trivial. This way of looking at the uses of noun phrases (whether in mathematics or elsewhere) brings out the difference between necessary and a priori truths even more sharply.

---

[5]Whether or not there are contingent a priori truths or necessary a posteriori truths is an open question and one that should have little to do with how we use our language; it should have to do with how the world is and with how agents might learn its many truths. Perhaps our most important means of acquiring information is through linguistic communication; not only that, much of the information we have could not be had without language. But the closer scrutiny initiated by Kripke himself should caution us against taking one of the relatively simple uses of language as evidence for rather startling claims about what are essentially ontological and epistemological concepts.

4.5 Singular Terms and Multiple Referents

As Barwise and Perry have emphasized, most accounts do not give adequate attention to the question of multiple referents for names and definite descriptions. From our situated perspective, solving this problem requires attending to the strategic efficiency of language, and once we see this as a key feature of the solution, the problem falls neatly into place with many of the other problems that we have considered above. Names and descriptions are efficient not only in that they can be used in different ways but also in their using the ambient circumstances to enable addressees to disambiguate possible ambiguities in their associated conditions. This problem of multiplicity is almost always with us when we consider indexicals like "here" or demonstratives like "this" or "that."

We will restrict our attention to the multiplicity problem for names. Our main example will involve a situation in which a name has two possible referents. We will briefly consider the case where the name in question has just one possible referent because it has some special features not shared by the more general case of multiple referents. We will also use the analysis of this problem to point to some of the new sets of questions that emerge from our model of situated communication.

Let's assume we have an environment $\mathfrak{E}$ in which there are precisely two Bills, Bill Smith and Bill Jones. We will look at different ways in which the sentence "Bill has the book" (call it φ) can be used by $\mathcal{A}$ to tell $\mathcal{B}$ that Bill Smith has the book. Call the proposition that Bill Smith has the book in question p. It is worth noting that even a simple sentence like this one requires many strategic inferences to get to the content p. First, the referring use of the name has to be inferred followed by an identification of the intended referent. Then, the same two problems have to be solved with "the book," figuring out its referential use and then identifying its referent. And the verb phrase "has the book" admits of many different readings because "has" is ambiguous. These five problems and more have to be solved *simultaneously* moreover, as a set of equations involved in the full communicative transfer of the content of the utterance.

For our more limited purposes in this section, we will simply assume that there is no problem in identifying the reference of "the book" and we will assume that "has" has the sense of "owns." Both these facts are to be common knowledge between $\mathcal{A}$ and $\mathcal{B}$. We also assume that it is common knowledge that "Bill" is being used referentially. (This abstracts from four of the five problems we mentioned above.)

Let us take the minimal content $m_d(\varphi)$ of an utterance of this sentence to be the proposition that someone named "Bill" has some book. Common knowledge of the reference of the noun phrase "the book" (by our assumption above) enables $\mathcal{A}$ and $\mathcal{B}$ to mutually establish the proposition that someone named "Bill" has the particular book assumed above. This intermediate proposition p_1 has more information than m_d but less information than p. Common knowledge of the sense of "has" as "owns" gets $\mathcal{A}$ and $\mathcal{B}$ to the proposition p_2 that someone named "Bill" owns that book. This is more informative than p_1, but it is still short of p. (We can order these propositions thus: $m_d \prec p_1 \prec p_2 \prec p$.) Our assumptions above imply that p_2 becomes common knowledge once $\mathcal{A}$ utters φ.

Our problem is to explore some ways in which the additional information, the proposition p that it is Bill Smith who has the book, gets communicated, and to show how the *SDM* provides a natural and fruitful way to model this flow of information.

A little reflection reveals that there is a staggering variety of utterance situations which make this transfer possible. There are all kinds of relevant facts that $\mathcal{A}$ and $\mathcal{B}$ might know or believe, they could share what they know to different degrees all the way up to having common knowledge of some of their private information, and each might have different sorts of goals that are all compatible with this transfer. And all this knowledge and information might have arisen in a bewildering number of ways. A common way (which itself provides many possibilities) is through previous discourse, or through complexes of discourse interwoven with other actions. There could be all sorts of (publicly) observable events going on around them. For example, Bill Smith might be physically present in the communication situation. Or $\mathcal{A}$ and $\mathcal{B}$ may be communicating by letter or by electronic mail and might not have access to the information that copresence provides. Not only this, we would need to distinguish between different ways in which this transfer might occur. Is the transfer a communicative one, or is it simply inferred from the strategic interaction that $\mathcal{A}$ and $\mathcal{B}$ participate in? There just are many different assumptions we could make about the discourse situation that suffice for the flow. Of course, we have assumed one constraint on all these possibilities and that is that all these utterances involve saying "Bill has the book." We could vary even this to look at the general problem of the conditions under which $\mathfrak{SDM}(\varphi, d, B) = p$ and p is communicatively transferred. (Also, there is our assumption that there are only two Bills in $\mathfrak{E}$. If we didn't assume this, then we would also have to take into account the possibility that only some part of p (more informative than p_2) might get through. For example, we could have a situation in which $\mathcal{A}$ succeeds in getting across to $\mathcal{B}$ that it is either Bill Smith or Bill Jones who has the book, not just any Bill.)

Our general problem then is to study a range of flows under different sets of assumptions on the circumstances (in which φ is uttered). We have given an extremely broad classification of the full range of flows or the full range of discourse situations that give rise to these flows. Flows are either communicative transfers or noncommunicative transfers depending on whether the *SDM* is a game or not. A finer-grained classification would have to come from our *SDM* itself. Though we will not actually provide this, the range of examples we consider will hint at what sorts of classes one might expect to discover.

An analogy is helpful at this point. In elementary mechanics we have the problem of studying the motion of a particle along a straight line. Once we specify the initial position and velocity of the particle and the resultant force that acts on the particle throughout its trajectory, we can use Newton's Second Law of Motion ($F = ma$) to predict its future course completely. Think of the proposition p as our particle and of the discourse situation d as our set of initial conditions. And think of the *SDM* as our Law of Motion. What we did in Chapter 2 was to study the "trajectory" of the strategic content under one set of initial conditions. We showed in fact that this content flows communicatively from $\mathcal{A}$ to $\mathcal{B}$. In mechanics we have a partial classification of different types of trajectories as being, say, oscillatory or of constant velocity. This classification is suggested by the Law of Motion and, in much the same way, the *SDM* ought to adumbrate the kinds of classes that are appropriate for studying the class of flows of information.

It is important to point out that what we are doing here is partially the inverse of what we did in Chapter 2. We could specify initial conditions and then ask for trajectories. Or we could specify trajectories and ask for initial conditions. The second problem is obviously much harder. Ideally, one would like a specification of the family of discourse situations (with or without φ held fixed) that succeed in communicating p. And we would like a specification of other types of discourse situations that succeed in just transferring p or perhaps communicating only some part of p and so on. We have given a partial solution to this problem through our definition of situated communication. The class of circumstances $\langle d, B \rangle$ that induce an *SDM* that is a game of partial information is precisely the class of circumstances that succeed in communicating p. (Of course, this definition is incomplete because we do not as yet have a definition of the class of all *SDM*s.) A general solution to this inverse problem would involve a classification of other types of strategic interactions, a game being an especially simple class.

This, (for reasons explained partially below), is beyond the scope of the tools we have at present. We have to be content with considering more or less arbitrary sets of initial conditions and solving the direct (rather than inverse) problem with the *SDM*. This is perhaps not too different from the situation in mechanics where only a few natural classes of trajectories can be identified, the full range of possible initial conditions being far too complex for taxonomic capture.

It is worthwhile to dwell just a little longer on this analogy and point out some ways in which our problem differs from the problem of one-dimensional motion. For one thing we do not as yet have a model that is as general as the Law of Motion. If this were possible and available, we would have a full technical vocabulary in terms of which to specify discourse situations the way we know that all we need to predict a particle trajectory is its initial position, velocity and the resultant force acting on it. This is one reason why going beyond our two types of flows is difficult at this stage of the game. Secondly, propositions are unlike particles in that they have "parts" and their parts can "travel" in relatively independent ways. This is something we alluded to above when we considered the different propositions m_d, p_1, p_2, and p. Only some part of p may be communicated or it may simply be transferred and so on. This makes specifying trajectories difficult.

Thirdly, a specific consequence of the Newtonian framework is that the relevant history of the particle's trajectory is fully captured by the two coordinates of position and velocity. In our case, it is quite unclear how history-independent the flow of propositions is. It appears that it is important to specify not only what an agent knows or what information he has but also how he came to know or possess it. One need only think about the complexities involved in anaphoric constructions to see this. In fact, flows of information, unlike particle trajectories, can depend on the future in complex ways as well. If A continued her utterance of "Every ten minutes a man gets mugged in New York" with "Today we are going to interview him," she would "cancel" the strategic inference that we discussed in Chapter 2, and convey the other proposition (that a particular man gets mugged every ten minutes) instead. All this is part of what makes the process of specifying suitable assumptions about discourse situations extremely difficult.

With these considerations in mind, let's look at some simple discourse situations. We will first consider a situation with just one possible referent and then go on to situations with multiple referents.

Let's start by assuming, temporarily, that there is only one Bill, Bill Smith, to refer to. How might an utterance of φ succeed in referring to, in being about Bill Smith? A simple sufficient condition on the discourse situation is that both $\mathcal{A}$ and $\mathcal{B}$ have common knowledge of the fact that there is only one Bill to refer to. Call this fact f. In this case $\mathcal{A}$ will succeed in referring to Smith and thus in communicating p. Call the proposition that $\mathcal{A}$ is referring to Smith q.

Would something "less than" common knowledge of f do? We could start by arguing that it is necessary for $\mathcal{B}$ to know f because without this, he would have no way to fix the reference of "Bill." This, it might seem, would do because if $\mathcal{A}$ says "Bill" then $\mathcal{B}$ can pick up (with the help of f) that it is Smith who is being referred to. But how is $\mathcal{A}$ to know this? And if she does not then she would have to, on rational grounds, opt for a different (and most likely, costlier) way to refer to Bill. Otherwise, though the information would get across to $\mathcal{B}$ it would not be communicated to $\mathcal{B}$. So, let's assume that $\mathcal{A}$ knows that $\mathcal{B}$ knows f. (This means of course that $\mathcal{A}$ must know f.) Since $\mathcal{A}$ knows that $\mathcal{B}$ can figure out the right reference, she will be able to rationally choose φ. And her saying φ will permit $\mathcal{B}$ to make the right inference and the attempt to communicate the reference will succeed. We need to make sure that p gets communicated, not just transferred. For this, we need only note that $\mathcal{B}$ has only one way to interpret "Bill" and the fact that $\mathcal{A}$ chose to say "Bill" gives $\mathcal{B}$ the inverse information that $\mathcal{A}$ knows that $\mathcal{B}$ knows f. And this is something that $\mathcal{A}$ can also inversely infer. In fact, $\mathcal{A}$ and $\mathcal{B}$ can get common knowledge of f and consequently of q, all by inverse interpretation, and this is why we get a communicative transfer of p.

The key fact in this flow is that $\mathcal{B}$ has no choice of interpretation. This is what allows a weaker condition than prior common knowledge of f to succeed. Even here, though, it works because it is possible for $\mathcal{A}$ and $\mathcal{B}$ to inversely infer common knowledge of f and q, thereby making the transfer a communicative one. This example suggests an important distinction for the class of (communicative) flows. Simpler communicative flows satisfy the requirements of common knowledge prior to the actual utterance, others satisfy it indirectly, partly through the inverse information that becomes publicly available as part of the public aspects of the utterance itself. $\mathcal{A}$ can count on $\mathcal{B}$'s using this publicly available inverse information to figure out the content even though the inverse information is not itself part of the content.

Now return to the situation $\mathfrak{E}$ in which there are two Bills. We can start by assuming that $\mathcal{A}$ is referring to Bill Smith when she says "Bill," that is, we can assume that q is true. Though this is natural it isn't really necessary. $\mathcal{A}$ might well choose to refer to Bill Jones and exploit some publicly shared constraint involving the two Bills, say that they own the same books. And this might allow $\mathcal{B}$ to infer that Bill Smith (also) has the book. To be sure, we would need to concoct a suitable narrative that would make this apparently strange behavior normal, that is, rational. But, given the wealth of ways in which people (and other agents) interact this should not be too difficult to author.

For the transfer to occur B needs to correctly infer who A is referring to. If he can do this, he will know who the particular use of "Bill" refers to and will therefore know that it is Bill Smith who has the book. It is reasonable to assume as we've done earlier that referential acts, like the communicative acts they help constitute, are not fully observable and the particular individual being referred to has to be typically inferred from other parts of the discourse situation.

Perhaps the simplest situation in which this transfer might occur is when B already happens to know p. We might start by assuming that it isn't common knowledge that B knows p. Otherwise A would have to be taken by B as communicating some proposition other than p (as an implicature). It may seem that if B knows p and A says φ then B should be able to infer that A is referring to Bill Smith and this would result in a transfer of p. However, there are many things that need to be considered before we can reach such a conclusion. It is possible, as far as B is concerned, that A wrongly believes that Bill Jones has the book, and that she is referring to Bill Jones as a result. Unless B knows that A has the information that p he cannot infer that A is referring to Smith. At best, he might conclude that A is probably conveying p (and even this would depend on what information he has to go on).

But this further assumption is still insufficient for A to have communicated p to B. We first need to be able to justify A's choosing to say φ if B already knows p. If A knows that B knows p then we would need to account for why A bothers to say φ at all. Perhaps she wants B to know that she knows p, in which case it is her knowing p rather than p itself that she might be getting across. But, as should be evident, unless B knows that A knows that B knows p, we can only say that her knowing p gets transferred, not communicated. And of course, A would need to know that B knows that A knows that B knows p, and so on to full public information of the fact that B knows p. And then, as we pointed out above, it would be some proposition other than p that gets communicated.

On the other hand, it may be the case that A does not know if B knows p. But then we would have to explain how A expected B to infer p, or prior to that, that she was referring to Smith. If A does not know that B knows p then A's optimal choice of sentence may have to be "Bill Smith has the book." The additional cost involved can be assumed to be less than the cost involved in leaving it ambiguous.

Or, more subtly perhaps, A might not care whether B can actually make the inference or not, as long as he gets the information that some Bill has the book. (She could still be referring to Smith, just in case B does manage to make the correct inference.) In this case too, even though B knows that A has the information he cannot legitimately infer that A is referring to Smith. This is because he is in the dark about what A's preferences are. And so here we would need to begin making assumptions about who knew what about A's preferences. But even if we did go all the way to common knowledge of A's preferences, we wouldn't get a case of communication because we are assuming that A does not know if B knows p. In fact, we would find again that it is better for A to say "Bill Smith has the book."

This should indicate how even in this seemingly simple discourse situation it is extremely difficult to solve the inverse problem, to provide necessary conditions for successful communication. The intricacies above should also convey at least a flavor of the kinds of nested and interconnected facts about knowledge and preferences that are involved in our communication problem. It is such facts that are captured by the relatively abstract condition that the circumstances be a game of partial information. This is why working with more complex structures of the kind provided by game theory (even if these need to be modified or generalized) is likely to be a more fruitful way to approach this problem than the more direct "toolless" approach adopted by Grice and Schiffer (1972). This hardly diminishes of course Grice's pioneering insights or their ingenuity in devising progressively more complex definitions. But game and strategic interaction theory appear equipped to do for the theory of communication (and of more general flows of information involving rational agents) what situation theory has done for the theory of information.

Let's drop the assumption that B already knows p. In this new utterance situation, we start by explicitly assuming first that A's goal is to communicate p to B. It is possible for p to flow from A to B without A's having this goal of course. A may simply want to tell B that one of the Bills has it (call this p_3) and B might already know that Bill Jones does not (and that there are only two Bills around). In this case, as with some of the cases above, we would be inclined to say that even though B is able to infer p from A's utterance, p has not really been communicated by A to B. (In fact, even p_3 does not get communicated in this case.)

We will assume next that it is common knowledge between A and B that there are just two Bills in $\mathfrak{C}$, Bill Smith and Bill Jones. And remember that we have already assumed that A is referring to Smith.

This much will succeed in communicating that one of the two Bills has the book. Note that anything less than public information of there being only two Bills will result in an uncommunicative transfer. We will continue to make this assumption in all the examples that follow unless explicitly stated otherwise.

What further assumptions might we make to get $\mathcal{A}$ to communicate p to $\mathcal{B}$? One possibility is to consider what $\mathcal{A}$ and $\mathcal{B}$ know about $\mathcal{A}$'s assumed goal. If this goal were already common knowledge between them no communication would be necessary. We could assume that $\mathcal{B}$ has some partial information about $\mathcal{A}$'s goal, say that $\mathcal{A}$ is communicating some information about Bill Smith, and that this partial information is common knowledge between them. This partial information can arise in many different ways. For example, $\mathcal{B}$ might have asked $\mathcal{A}$ prior to $\mathcal{A}$'s utterance what Bill Smith has.

This set of assumptions, that $\mathcal{A}$'s goal is to communicate p to $\mathcal{B}$, that it is common knowledge between them that $\mathcal{A}$ wants to convey some information about Bill Smith, that there are two possible Bills to refer to and that this is also common knowledge between them, and finally that $\mathcal{A}$ is referring to Smith, gives us the first utterance situation we will explicitly model using our *SDM*. These assumptions make up our set of Circumstantial Assumptions. It is important to mention that these assumptions can come about in a wide range of ways. In other words, this set of sufficient conditions covers many different kinds of situations. In terms of our analogy above, this gives us an instance of a situation in which these conditions serve to summarize all the relevant history of the utterance situation, as did information about position, velocity, and force for particle trajectories.

We consider the relevant local game $LG(\varphi)$ for this utterance situation below. Call the proposition that $\mathcal{A}$ is referring to Bill Jones q'. Let ψ_1 be the sentence "Bill Smith has the book" and ψ_2 be the sentence "Bill Jones has the book."

We need to make a small modification in the *SDM* as we defined it in Chapter 3. The initial situations in local games were communicative situations containing *soas* of the type $\sigma_{itc}(p)$. When we consider subsentential expressions we need to consider different sorts of initial situations. In our case, we need to consider what we will call *referential situations*. A referential situation contains an *soa* of the type $\langle\!\langle\, ref, \mathcal{A}, o, \alpha \,\rangle\!\rangle$ where *ref* is the three-place relation of an agent $\mathcal{A}$ referring to some object o with the expression α. We can define the function σ_{ref} with domain $A \times \mathfrak{L}$ and codomain SOA such that $\sigma_{ref}(o, \alpha) = \langle\!\langle\, ref, \mathcal{A}, o, \alpha \,\rangle\!\rangle$. And correspondingly, we can define the function r with domain $A \times \mathfrak{L}$

and codomain SIT such that $r(o, \alpha) = \{\sigma_{ref}(o, \alpha)\}$.[6] Let BS stand for Bill Smith and BJ for Bill Jones in Figure 4.6.

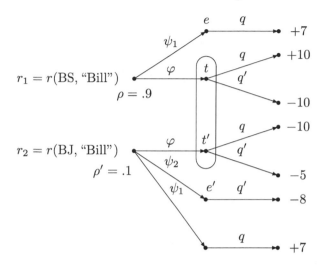

FIGURE 4.6 Reference – Example 1

Strictly speaking, the two initial situations are more complex than we have indicated. Instead of the simple situation r_1 we should have a disjunctive situation of the type $\{\langle\langle or, \sigma_{ref}(\text{BS}, \text{"Bill Smith"}),$ $\sigma_{ref}(\text{BS}, \text{"Bill"})\rangle\rangle\}$. That is, the initial referential situation is one in which the speaker is referring to BS either with "Bill Smith" or with just "Bill." The "or" is a disjunction relation between the two *soas*. Similarly, the second initial situation r_2 contains the *soa* $\langle\langle or,$ $\sigma_{ref}(\text{BJ}, \text{"Bill Jones"}), \sigma_{ref}(\text{BJ}, \text{"Bill"}), \sigma_{ref}(\text{BS}, \text{"Bill Smith"})\rangle\rangle$. In this situation, we have the additional *soa* in which $\mathcal{A}$ is referring to BS with "Bill Smith." We have omitted this to keep things simple. The key difference between the two initial situations is that "Bill" is used differently in them, if it is used. The choice before $\mathcal{A}$ is to decide what name to utter given the referential choices available to her.

Further, the actions indicated should be subsentential utterances, of the respective names. However, we will stick to the whole sentences just for notational convenience. Most of the payoffs are obvious. We need to explain the -5 and -8. Here $\mathcal{B}$ makes the correct inference that

---

[6]It is of course possible to refer to objects other than individuals and the correct domain for these two functions is O rather than A multiplied with $\mathcal{L}$. Also, since we are considering subsentential expressions α we should extend $\mathcal{L}$ to include such expressions as well.

$\mathcal{A}$ is referring to Bill Jones (relative to the initial situation $r(\text{BJ}, \text{"Bill"})$),
but this leads to the further conclusion that $\mathcal{A}$ is communicating the
proposition that Bill Jones has the book, which $\mathcal{B}$ knows is incompatible
with their assumed prior common knowledge that $\mathcal{A}$ is communicating
some information about Bill Smith. So, though one inference is correct,
the other one isn't and we assign that a payoff of -5. And similarly for
the -8, except that we now have to add in an additional cost for the
costlier utterance ψ_2. Note that in the case where the initial situation
is $r(\text{BJ}, \text{"Bill"})$ and the path is $\langle \varphi, q \rangle$ we have assigned a payoff of -10.
Here, the primary inference that $\mathcal{A}$ is referring to Bill Smith by uttering
"Bill" is wrong (relative to $r(\text{BJ}, \text{"Bill"})$) even though the further inference that p is being communicated is correct. The particular values we
assign don't really matter as long as they are all less than the payoff
obtained by uttering ψ_1 in that situation.

As a game it is trivial to solve. The single Nash equilibrium of the
game is clearly $\{(r_1, \varphi), (r_2, \psi_1); (\{t, t'\}, q)\}$. The interpretation of this
solution is that $\mathcal{A}$ chooses φ in r_1 and ψ_1 in r_2. And $\mathcal{B}$ chooses q at
his information set. (This solution is consistent with the global game
because it includes φ. We do not bother to draw the tree for the global
game because it is trivial.)

Note that we have not treated referential acts as choices available
to the speaker. In a more complete model we should include two choices
for the speaker, one of who or what to refer to, and second, of what
expression to utter to communicate that choice.

This completes our analysis of the first utterance situation. For
our next utterance situation let's consider some of the possibilities that
arise when $\mathcal{B}$ has even less partial information about $\mathcal{A}$'s goal. We have
already assumed that they share common knowledge of the fact that
there are only two possible Bills to refer to. When $\mathcal{B}$ perceives φ, he
will be able to infer the proposition p_3 that one of the two Bills has the
book. (Note that p_3 is more informative than p_2, but it is still short of
p. This is yet another "part" of the informational "particle" p.) Because
it is publicly known between them that there are only two Bills around
we can say here that p_3 gets communicated to $\mathcal{B}$. And this allows $\mathcal{B}$ to
infer some partial information about $\mathcal{A}$'s goal as inverse information.
The partial information is that $\mathcal{A}$ wants to convey some information
about one of the two Bills. $\mathcal{A}$ knows that $\mathcal{B}$ can make this inference,
and in fact, this partial information about $\mathcal{A}$'s goal becomes common
knowledge between them.

In the absence of any further information, there is little more that
$\mathcal{B}$ can do. We could assume that $\mathcal{A}$ and $\mathcal{B}$ have common knowledge of
the fact that Smith is much more likely to have the book. Perhaps Bill

Smith is the bibliophile. It is important to point out that this information about probabilities can arise in many different ways. In the case mentioned above where Bill Smith is the book lover this information would have to be inferred jointly from Bill's amatory inclinations and from the rest of the sentence, that is, from the verb phrase "has the book." If the sentence had been a different one, say "Bill is having breakfast," Smith's love of books would have nothing to contribute to the flow. We also need to assume that there are no other factors that might lead $\mathcal{A}$ to refer to Jones.

Here, too, nothing short of common knowledge of this high probability that $\mathcal{A}$ is referring to Smith will do. But if these conditions are satisfied we can show that p does get communicated to $\mathcal{B}$. And besides, $\mathcal{B}$ will be able to infer $\mathcal{A}$'s goal inversely and this goal will be publicly available to them for later use. This, then, is our second utterance situation.

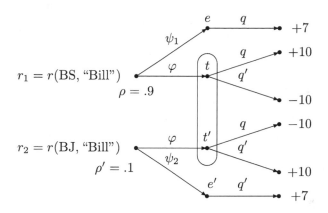

FIGURE 4.7 Reference – Example 2

In the game depicted in Figure 4.7, $\mathcal{B}$ does not have even partial knowledge of the speaker's goal and this makes the payoffs symmetric. This game is identical to the one we considered in Chapter 2.

We conclude this section with a few observations. Our examples above were all couched in terms of agents knowing this or that. But essentially the same (sort of) analysis would hold for the weaker condition of their believing the corresponding facts. And beliefs offer some interesting possibilities that knowledge does not. For example, in many cases, it may suffice for $\mathcal{A}$ and $\mathcal{B}$ to have a mutual belief that something is the case without it actually being so. Bill Smith may always have been seen by $\mathcal{A}$ and $\mathcal{B}$ with books and jointly concluded that he was a bibliophile even though this might simply be his way of working out. Bill Smith may not even be Bill Smith and yet a mutual belief to this effect will suffice to mutually establish the correct referent! (Here is a natural informative use of what would be considered a contradictory sentence by most theories.) And weaker conditions yet will also suffice. What is needed in many cases is not mutual belief but mutual belief that one of the two agents has a certain belief. This ties in with some of our observations in earlier sections. Another consideration is that with beliefs issues about the strength of various beliefs (probabilities) would play an important role.

Similar analyses would go through for other singular terms as well. Thus, the problem of multiple referents is just another instance of the efficiency of situated communication.

In a more complete analysis, we would have to consider not just the problem of multiplicity but also the problems of figuring out how a singular term is being used and what the resource situation is, if needed. Not only that, to analyze a complete utterance we would need to consider all the strategic inferences involved simultaneously.

4.6 Conclusion

We have looked at a number of different kinds of applications of the *SDM*. In particular, we looked at a new account of names and descriptions that the *SDM* makes possible. It appears safe to conclude that strategic inferences and the situated game-theoretic structures they embody play a fundamental role in the structures involved in the communication of information.

5

Conclusion

We have shown, in the preceding chapters, how communication and other types of information flows can be modeled by a situation-and-game-theoretic structure called the Strategic Discourse Model.

Perhaps the most important consequence of this model is that it gives us necessary and sufficient conditions for communication. A transfer of information between two rational agents is a communication if and only if the *SDM* is a situated game of partial information. We can, if we wish, choose to *define* communication by this condition. It should be possible then to derive the conditions imposed by Grice (1969), Strawson (1964), and Schiffer (1972) in a precise way, as consequences or theorems. In order to do this, we would need first to give a more general definition of the class of *SDM*s that includes strategic interactions that are not games. We analyzed one such example in detail to illustrate the kinds of complexities involved. In its current state, game theory does not in fact have examples or definitions of these more general interactions in which common knowledge of the structure is not assumed.

The content communicated is given by the Pareto-Nash equilibrium of the game. This provides a precise method for determining the content of an utterance. We expressed some dissatisfaction about the current theory of solutions in game theory. Though there have been many sophisticated and subtle analyses of this problem, we are still short of a satisfactory theory. We used the concept of a Pareto-Nash equilibrium in a relatively cavalier way, without deriving it from first principles, and this would be an important problem to address in further developments of the *SDM*.

The *SDM* gives us a method for deriving what might be called the fundamental equation of semantics from more basic assumptions. The equation is $\mathfrak{SDM}_{\mathfrak{L}}(\varphi, d, B) = \mathcal{C}$, where φ is the sentence uttered, d the discourse situation, B the background, and C the set of communicated contents. $\mathfrak{SDM}_{\mathfrak{L}}$ is the mapping that takes us from meanings to contents, relative to a language $\mathfrak{L}$. The model we develop is a first step in this direction. A complete SDM would incorporate all the strategic inferences involved in a complete utterance. Mathematically, this would be a system of simultaneous equations. This simultaneous equation idea offers the most promising avenue for further development of the SDM. It is indeed possible to develop an even more general model of communication and of this equation by treating the language $\mathfrak{L}$ itself as a variable, rather than as a fixed parameter. We have a partial formulation of such a model in Parikh (1987).[1]

An important consequence of the model we have developed here is that communication is situated. This fact makes it possible for the speaker and addressee to communicate with very simple first-order intentions, unlike the infinitely nested ones postulated by Grice, Strawson, and Schiffer. The ambient game provides the rest of the structure. This parallels Perry's (1986a) observations about situated beliefs. Situated communication, as an interaction between two agents, is efficient in the same way as the situated action of a single agent.

Another important consequence of our analysis is that the shared language used by the speaker and addressee affects the content communicated in direct and indirect ways. Directly, of course, the language constrains one to choose from a class of sentences. Indirectly, this choice plays a subtler and equally important role because the content communicated depends not just on what sentence was uttered but also on what sentences might have been uttered but were not. It is this element that, in addition to the more obvious roles played by beliefs and intentions, makes strategic inferences and therefore communication have the range and power they have.

We pointed out several ways in which the SDM could be improved. One relatively straightforward extension is to consider mixed strategies and probabilistic inferences. In this more general case, the fundamental equation we discussed above would also need to be generalized. The set of communicated contents C would be transferred together with a probability distribution on this set. That is, the appropriate object to consider is a set of propositions with an accompanying probability distribution, not just a proposition. (We are, of course, ignoring the illocutionary force of the utterance here which is a critical part of the content and one which we considered in some detail in Chapter 2.)

---

[1]This is essentially a general equilibrium model of language and communication in the tradition of Arrow and Debreu.

There are several other interesting modifications we suggested. We do not repeat these here; we simply mention them as interesting directions for further exploration. As we said in Chapter 1, our hope and principal effort has been to combine ideas from two quite different disciplines and styles of thought in order to develop tools, indeed a language, for studying the various problems connected with the concept of communication, and the flow of information more generally.

As our main application we sketched a new theory of names and descriptions. For this we needed, in addition to the rationality or communicative constraint represented by the *SDM*, the idea of an informational or ontological constraint. Our main claim here was that it was these two constraints working together that enabled one to go from the meaning of a name or description to its content in a given utterance. A central consequence of this analysis was a semantical relation between the linguistic item (whether name or description) and the bit of the world it is about in a particular use. This relation appears to provide something like a tentative step toward a more general theory of linguistic representation.

Our account also provides a new and, we hope, clearer way to see the traditional referential-attributive distinction. Essentially, this distinction is analogous to the distinction between two different ways we have of specifying sets, by explicit enumeration or by the method of abstraction. The referential use is like enumeration and the attributive use like the method of abstraction. Just as there are two standard ways of specifying sets, so there are two ways of specifying individuals. In addition to these, we describe other ways of using descriptions.

The theory suggests that the number of ways of using an expression is given by the number of logically or informationally possible permutations permitted by our ontology. Essentially, every linguistic item is circumstantially (i.e. strategically) associated with a property, and a property can be ontologically transformed into other related entities like its (situation-relative) instantiations or extensions in a fixed number of ways. This number is fixed insofar as the logical properties of properties are fixed.

An interesting consequence of our theory is that it provides a new way of looking at many of the puzzles that are traditionally associated with names and descriptions. We briefly consider the problem of existential statements and then show, in some detail, how the Fregean riddle of informative identity statements can be solved on our approach. Both solutions involve the insight that names and descriptions can be used in a number of ontologically and communicatively constrained ways. Once we adopt this economics of action approach, most such puzzles can be handled in a simple and unified manner. Our account also explains how apparently contradictory statements, like "The butler did it, but the butler isn't the butler," can be quite informative if executed appropriately.

An important feature of our account is that names are in essence no different from descriptions in how they work. The theory we sketch gives a unified picture of names and descriptions, one moreover that can be easily generalized to wider classes of expressions. This is important because it is a simpler account that does not require different mechanisms for different expressions. In particular, there does not seem to be any evidence that precludes such a mechanism for names.

Language is a remarkably flexible tool for communicating information. The theory of names and descriptions we outline shows in a relatively precise way how some of this flexibility comes about. We spell this out in some detail in looking at a part of this problem. We show under what conditions successful reference can occur. This problem turns out to be structurally similar to the problem of disambiguating an utterance that we consider in an earlier chapter. Reference is successful when it is communicated and the necessary and sufficient conditions for successful reference are thus the same as those for communication.

As we pointed out in Chapter 1, our approach should have interesting consequences for other types of information transfers as well, in particular for the problems of ambiguity, implicatures, and direct and indirect speech acts. If we combine these results with our definition of communication, we get a new and more precise way to see the connection between Grice's idea of nonnatural meaning and his idea of implicatures.

Situation theory, game theory, and their combination appear to be quite fruitful ways of dealing with a wide range of problems connected with the study of information and mind. We hope the analysis presented here provides a partial vindication of this claim.

References

Peter Aczel. *Non-Well-Founded Sets*. CSLI Publications, Stanford, 1988.

Kenneth Arrow. *The Limits of Organization*. Norton, New York, 1974.

R. J. Aumann. What is game theory trying to accomplish? In Kenneth Arrow and Seppo Honkapohja, editors, *Frontiers of Economics*. Oxford Blackwell, 1985.

Robert J. Aumann. Lectures on Game Theory. Based on lectures delivered at Stanford University, 1976.

Robert J. Aumann. Correlated equilibrium as an expression of Bayesian rationality. *Econometrica*, 55:1–18, 1987.

J. L. Austin. Performative utterances. In *Philosophical Papers*. Oxford University Press, Oxford, third edition, 1961/1979. Edited by J. O. Urmson and G. J. Warnock.

J. L. Austin. *How To Do Things With Words*. Harvard University Press, Cambridge, Massachusetts, second edition, 1975. Edited by J. O. Urmson and Marina Sbisa.

Jon Barwise. On the model theory of common knowledge. In *The Situation in Logic*. CSLI Publications, Stanford, 1989a.

Jon Barwise. Logic and information. In *The Situation in Logic*. CSLI Publications, Stanford, 1989b. First appeared as "The Situation in Logic–I," in *Logic, Methodology, and the Philosophy of Science VII*, ed. B. Marcus (Amsterdam: North-Holland, 1983).

Jon Barwise. Conditionals and conditional information. In *The Situation in Logic*. CSLI Publications, Stanford, 1989c. First appeared in *On Conditionals*, ed. E. C. Traugott, A. ter Meulen, J. S. Reilly, and C. A. Ferguson (Cambridge: Cambridge University Press, 1986).

Jon Barwise. Situations, sets, and the axiom of foundation. In *The Situation in Logic*. CSLI Publications, Stanford, 1989d.

Jon Barwise and John Etchemendy. *The Liar*. Oxford University Press, London, 1986.

Jon Barwise and John Perry. Semantic innocence and uncompromising situations. In Peter French, Theodore Uehling Jr., and Howard Wettstein, editors, *Midwest Studies in Philosophy: The Foundations of Analytic Philosophy*, volume 6, pages 387–403. University of Minnesota Press, 1975.

Jon Barwise and John Perry. *Situations and Attitudes*. The MIT Press, Cambridge, Massachusetts, 1983.

B. D. Bernheim. Rationalizeable strategic behaviour. *Econometrica*, 52: 1007–1028, 1984.

A. Brandenburger and E. Dekel. Rationalizeability and correlated equilibria. Unpublished preprint, Stanford University and Harvard University, 1985.

T. Burge. Reference and proper names. *Journal of Philosophy*, 73, 1973.

In-Koo Cho and David Kreps. Signaling games and stable equilibria. *The Quarterly Journal of Economics*, 102(2):179–222, 1987.

Herbert H. Clark and Catherine R. Marshall. Definite reference and mutual knowledge. In Joshi, Webber, and Sag, editors, *Elements of Discourse Understanding*. Cambridge University Press, 1981.

Keith Donnellan. Reference and definite descriptions. *Philosophical Review*, 75:281–304, 1966.

Fred I. Dretske. *Knowledge and the Flow of Information*. The MIT Press, Cambridge, Massachusetts, 1981.

Herbert B. Enderton. *Elements of Set Theory*. Academic Press, Florida, 1977.

G. Evans. The causal theory of names. *Aristotelian Society Supplementary Volume*, 47:187–208, 1973.

Gottlob Frege. On sense and meaning. In Peter Geach and Max Black, editors, *Translations from the Philosophical Writings of Gottlob Frege*, pages 56–78. Basil Blackwell Ltd., 1892/1980.

H. P. Grice. Meaning. *Philosophical Review*, 66:377–388, 1957.

H. P. Grice. Utterer's meaning, sentence-meaning and word-meaning. *Foundations of Language*, 4:1–18, 1968.

H. P. Grice. Utterer's meaning and intentions. *Philosophical Review*, 78: 147–177, 1969.

H. P. Grice. Logic and conversation. In Peter Cole and Jerry L. Morgan, editors, *Syntax and Semantics*, volume 3, pages 41–58. Academic Press, New York, 1975.

J. C. Harsanyi. Games with incomplete information played by Bayesian players. *Management Science*, 14:159–182, 320–334, 486–502, 1967.

W. C. Kneale. Universality and necessity. *British Journal for the Philosophy of Science*, 12, 1962.

Elon Kohlberg and Jean-François Mertens. On the strategic stability of equilibria. *Econometrica*, 54(5):1003–1037, September 1986.

David Kreps. Out of equilibrium beliefs and out of equilibrium behavior. Working Paper, Graduate School of Business, Stanford University, 1986.

David Kreps and Garey Ramey. Structural consistency, consistency and sequential rationality. *Econometrica*, 55:1331–1348, July 1987.

David Kreps and Robert Wilson. Sequential equilibrium. *Econometrica*, 50: 863–894, July 1982.

Saul Kripke. Speaker's reference and semantic reference. In Peter A. French, Theodore E. Uehling Jr., and Howard K. Wettstein, editors, *Contemporary Perspectives in the Philosophy of Language*, pages 6–27. University of Minnesota Press, 1977.

Saul Kripke. *Naming and Necessity*. Harvard University Press, Cambridge, Massachusetts, 1980.

David Lewis. *Convention*. Harvard University Press, Cambridge, Massachusetts, 1969.

David Lewis. Language and languages. In Keith Gunderson, editor, *Language, Mind, and Knowledge*, pages 3–35. University of Minnesota Press, 1975.

L. Linsky. *Referring*. Routledge and Kegan Paul, London, 1967.

A. P. Martinich. *Communication and Reference*. Walter de Gruyter, Berlin and New York, 1984.

J. Nash. Non-cooperative games. *Annals of Mathematics*, 54:286–295, 1951.

Prashant Parikh. Conventional meaning and equilibrium. Unpublished, 1987.

Prashant Parikh. *Communication and Content*. Language Science Press, Berlin, 2019.

Barbara H. Partee. Noun phrase interpretation and type-shifting principles. In Jeroen Groenendijk, Dick de Jongh, and Martin Stokhof, editors, *Studies in Discourse Representation Theory and the Theory of Generalized Quantifiers*, pages 115–143. Dordrecht, Holland, 1986.

John Perry. Circumstantial attitudes and benevolent cognition. Technical Report No. CSLI-86-53, CSLI, Stanford University, 1986a.

John Perry. Thought without representation. *Aristotelean Society Supplementary Volume*, 60:137–151, 1986b.

Bertrand Russell. *Introducton to Mathematical Philosophy*, chapter Descriptions, pages 167–180. George Allen and Unwin Publishers Ltd., 1919.

T. C. Schelling. *The Strategy of Conflict*. Harvard University Press, Cambridge, Massachusetts, 1960.

Stephen Schiffer. *Meaning*. Oxford University Press, Oxford, 1972.

John Searle. *Intentionality*. Cambridge University Press, Cambridge, UK, 1983.

John R. Scarle. Proper names. *Mind*, 67:166–173, 1958.

John R. Searle. Metaphor. In A. Ortony, editor, *Metaphor and Thought*, pages 92–123. Cambridge University Press, Cambridge, UK, 1979.

P. F. Strawson. On referring. In Antony Flew, editor, *Essays in Conceptual Analysis*, pages 21–52. MacMillan and Co. Ltd., London, 1956.

P. F. Strawson. Intention and convention in speech acts. *Philosophical Review*, 73:439–460, 1964.

P. F. Strawson. 'If' and '⊃'. In Richard Grandy and Richard Warner, editors, *Philosophical Grounds of Rationality*, pages 229–242. Clarendon Press, Oxford, 1986.

Index

Printed in the United States
By Bookmasters